CLEARING THE BASES

BILL STARR

CLEARING THE BASES

Baseball Then & Now

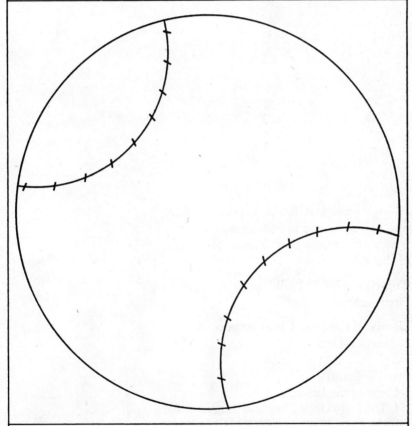

 MICHAEL KESEND PUBLISHING, LTD.
NEW YORK

To
Norman, Philip, Marsha and Harvey

Copyright 1989 © by Bill Starr
First publication 1989

Library of Congress Cataloging-in-
Publication Data

Starr, Bill, 1911–
  Clearing the bases.
  1. Baseball—United States—History. I. Title.
GV863.A1S8 1989 796.357'0973 88-32847
ISBN 0-935576-30-4

c.1

C O N T E N T S

Acknowledgments   vii

Foreword   ix

Introduction   xv

1. After the Scandal   1

2. Faster, Bigger, Stronger—FBS, as in FIBS   11

3. The Myth of the Lively Ball   20

4. Baseball's Most Durable, Most Overlooked Record   37

5. The Strikeout—Baseball's Most Positive Negative   48

6. The Minor Leagues, 1920–1949   64

7. Attitudes in the 1920s and 1930s   80

8. Knockdowns, Brushbacks, and Pitching   90

9. Fundamentals—What Are They Talking About?   99

10. How Johnny Bench Ruined the Art of Catching   116

11. The Balk Rule—the Umpires' True Love   125

12. Computerball Statistics Are Bullshit!   136

13. Behind the Scenes   154

Index   163

ACKNOWLEDGMENTS

My first step in this venture was a visit to the San Diego public libraries. This promptly validated my doubts about the theory of the self-made man. There's no such animal.

I relearned a fact that I'm ashamed to admit was once known to me but forgotten: Public libraries are indispensable institutions, the greatest sources of information on every conceivable subject, including baseball. The library card is the most valuable card a person can carry, and at the price of one dollar, the best buy on earth. I found baseball books and records that I needed and never knew existed. A big thank-you to Sydney Stanley, senior librarian of the Mission Hills branch of the San Diego libraries, for being there when I needed her. Count me as a lifetime advocate and supporter of the San Diego libraries.

I owe a special debt to all the ex-players, the managers, and executives without whose input this book would never have been accomplished (or undertaken). My discussions with them began in 1984 and, with some of them, continued into early 1988. During this interim, the baseball world and I have been saddened by the deaths of some wonderful people, great and famous ex-players who participated in my undertaking. I think of my correspondence, interviews, and discussions with Hank Greenberg, Glenn Wright, Ossie Bluege, Jigger Statz, Babe Herman, and Wally Berger. It was not easy for them to be subjected to the questions I asked and the long conversations my questions engendered. Yet they never protested. In fact, I sensed their interest and even their desire to cooperate in my project. I am indebted to them.

I am equally indebted to Jimmie Reese, Ralph Kiner, Al Lopez, Johnny Kerr, Willie Kamm, Bibb Falk, Ferris Fain, Bob Lemon, Sparky Anderson, and Buzzie Bavasi for their contributions.

I suppose I should thank Howard Chernoff for pushing me into this four-year project. He should bear the responsibility for his indiscretion. I am also indebted to William Weber Johnson, Naneen Van Gelder, and Charles Champlin for their professional guidance and encouragement. My gratitude to Earl Keller, Mil Chipp, Lowell Reidenbaugh, and the research staff of the Hall of Fame Museum in Cooperstown for researching and furnishing me with the statistical data I needed.

I am grateful to Michael Kesend of Michael Kesend Publishing, Ltd., for his confidence in my work and his guidance throughout. To Mel Minter, who edited this book, how can I repay his efforts in shaping up my work? I thank Ellen Beach, who did all the typing and abided my intrusions with never a complaint. To anyone I may have overlooked, please forgive my oversight. Attribute it to my lack of memory pills.

I suppose I also owe something to my son, Philip, who holds a degree in linguistics. I sent him an early rough draft of my manuscript and got back a quick reply that made me regret my investment in his education. He wrote: "Dad, the word oxymoron is not in your vocabulary. Leave it to Bill Buckley. It's his property."

So how do I explain Branch Rickey's confusing comment that baseball is a scientific art? That sounds like the equivalent of a married bachelor.

And a big hug to my wife, Francy, a former high-school teacher who can grasp a sentence in midflight, rearrange the tenses, remove the qualifiers, reorganize the clauses, and hand it back to you as a finished product before you can say: "Hold the English lesson."

For this foreword I located a newspaper item that I recall reading about Bill Starr in early 1956.

He had been the principal owner of the San Diego Padres in the Pacific Coast League for the previous eleven years and had just sold his club to a San Diego bank. I had retired a few months earlier as a player with Cleveland, when the bank called. Would I be interested in taking over Bill's job as the chief operating officer of the club? I certainly would.

Shortly thereafter, an item appeared in a column by Jack Murphy, the nationally prominent sports editor of the *San Diego Union*, for whom the ball park in San Diego is now named. Jack was interviewing Leslie O'Connor, who had come into baseball in 1919 as an assistant to Commissioner Landis, continuing his career as special assistant to Commissioner "Happy" Chandler and finally as a lawyer for the major leagues and the Pacific Coast League. The interview turned to the subject of Bill Starr, and here is Murphy's comment and O'Connor's quote:

> O'Connor was especially outspoken in his admiration for Bill Starr. "To my notion," says O'Connor, "Bill Starr was the keenest mind in baseball. Nobody was a better judge of playing talent and he was unsurpassed as a negotiator. When I say he was the smartest man in baseball, I don't exclude anybody. I rate him over George Weiss of the Yankees, over Frank Lane of the Cardinals, over all of 'em."

My reaction to reading that was—Wow! Better than all of them? That would include Bill Veeck and even Branch Rickey. Starr was given enough of a tribute to last a lifetime. Am I expected to follow that guy?

About then Bill and I started a friendship that has lasted to this day. During this interval of 32 years, I have found no reason to dispute O'Connor's views. Bill had a not too illustrious career as a catcher, almost entirely in the minor leagues. I soon learned that what he lacked as a player was many times compensated by his expertise as a baseball executive. He was involved in every aspect of the baseball business. He discovered, developed, and sold player talent to the major leagues. In 1953 he sold Tom Alston to the St. Louis Cardinals for the largest price ever paid for a minor league player in history—$125,000 and four players valued at another $50,000. These players helped win the pennant for the Padres the next year.

Bill provided the leadership that guided the Coast League through the turbulent years of dispute with the major leagues. He was a pioneer and an innovator. In 1948 he opened the doors to black players in the Coast League by acquiring John Ritchey, the first black player to play in that league's history. In 1952, a dozen years before Branch Rickey caught up with the idea, Bill advocated and designed a central scouting system for the Pacific Coast League, which the league didn't adopt—to its subsequent regret. Twenty-five years later, major league clubs embraced a central scouting system.

Now that I have read his book, *Clearing the Bases*, I wonder what praise I can add to O'Connor's tribute to him. Bill has written a book that every professional in baseball or dedicated fan of the game will understand and enjoy, even if some may not agree with all of his views. Although on the surface his book may appear to be an argument for the good old days versus current-day baseball, that is not what this book is about. It is basically a serious work, the most informative, most penetrating book on baseball that I ever read. It is also peppered with many amusing experiences. I cracked up reading about a wonderful old-timer, Herman "Old Folks" Pillette, who was a teammate of Bill Starr's on the 1937 Padres.

When Bill writes about the tendency of the media and fans to connect baseball with football and basketball, he makes a valid point in linking baseball instead with golf, tennis, and hockey.

I admit that until I read his book, I always believed and was quoted that the .303 batting average achieved by the National League in 1930 had to be the result of a juiced-up baseball. His chapters "The Myth of the Lively Ball" and "Baseball's Most Durable, Most Overlooked Record" changed my mind, as it will or should with everyone else. I never realized the concentration of talent that played in the majors in 1930. Thirty-seven Hall of Fame players, in their prime, on only 16 teams, all in 1 year! That is *twice* as many Hall of Famers in 1 year as all the Hall of Famers during my *10* years in the big leagues. Will we ever total 37 superstars again in 1 year, even with 26 teams? Seems impossible.

When he writes about the damaging effects of strikeouts, I know what he is saying, based upon my own experience. In 1946, my first year with Pittsburgh, I hit 23 homers and had a league-leading 109 strikeouts, with a .247 batting average. The next year it was my good fortune to have Hank Greenberg join our club. We became roommates and the closest of friends. He taught me how to concentrate on the strike zone, how to avoid chasing bad balls. The result: I reduced my strikeouts by 35 percent, increased my homers to 51, and averaged .313.

Bill Starr doesn't believe that to achieve home runs you have to pay for it with an excessive number of strikeouts—that you can't have the benefit of one without the penalty of the other. I totally agree. What he deplores are strikeouts induced by swinging at bad balls, whether by home run hitters or singles hitters. This bad habit is the result of a variety of factors that are described by veteran players interviewed for his book.

Bill Starr is 78 years old. I suspect that some readers may characterize his book as a trip into nostalgia. If so, they will be misjudging him and his book. I can prove it. From 1947 through 1955, in the National League, I played against Jackie Robinson, Roy Campanella, Pee Wee Reese, Gil Hodges, Enos Slaughter, Johnny Mize, Stan Musial, Willie Mays, Duke Snider, Eddie Mathews, Ernie Banks, Hank Aaron, Roberto Clemente, and pitchers such as Warren Spahn, Robin Roberts, Ewell Blackwell, Johnny Sain, Sal Maglie, and Johnny Vander Meer. In the American League, there were players during that period such as Joe DiMaggio, Mickey Mantle, Phil Rizzuto, Yogi Berra, Ted Williams, Bobby Doerr, Lou Boudreau, Larry Doby, Al Kaline, and pitchers Whitey Ford, Allie Reynolds, Hal Newhouser, Herb Score, Bob Feller, Bob Lemon, and Early Wynn. Most of these players are in the Hall of Fame. Many of the others will make it in the veteran's section of the Hall of Fame. Now, if I were to state that these were some of the greatest players ever to put on a uniform, I don't think there would be a single person who would disagree with me, much less accuse me of indulging in nostalgia. Yet, I'm going back 33 to 41 years ago. In 1956, when Bill Starr first talked to me about the talent of the players of the twenties and thirties, he was going back only 17 to 36 years. He was but 45 years old then. In *Clearing the Bases*, he is now repeating views that he has held since 1956, to my knowledge, and undoubtedly long before then. How can that be nostalgia?

I can explain what is happening. There are not many fans around today who have seen the players of the twenties and thirties. I haven't. But there are many fans who have seen the players I named. Ten, 20, or 30 years from now, my list of players will dim in memory. New, outstanding players will be swinging hot bats and making remarkable defensive plays. And should I be around touting my old list of players, that's when I, too, will be accused of giving in to nostalgia.

It will be quickly evident to any reader that a tremendous

amount of new information on baseball went into this book. Bill
Starr analyzes baseball as a professional, disclosing insights into
the game that are rarely considered by or revealed to the fans.
He's had access to the views of numerous professional baseball
players and managers—from Jigger Statz, whose experience went
back to 1919, to Sparky Anderson, a current-day manager.

How good was baseball in the twenties and thirties? I don't
know. That was before my time. But I have talked to players of
that era such as Charlie Gehringer, Joe Sewell, Bill Dickey, and
others. And, of course, with my close friend Hank Greenberg
who once said to me: "Do you know that in all my years in baseball I was never elected to the All-Star team?" I could hardly believe
it. Everyone knows what a great player Greenberg was. His problem: ahead of him were Lou Gehrig and Jimmie Foxx, with Hal
Trosky not far behind. Baseball must have been pretty good in
the thirties to have four first basemen such as Gehrig, Foxx,
Greenberg, and Trosky in one league at the same time.

Although *Clearing the Bases* does not compare individual
players or teams from one period of time to those of another,
its emphasis on the twenties and thirties gives the impression that
baseball was best in those days. I'm not sure those were baseball's
best years. Naturally, I think my era of 1947 through 1955 was
best. Others may insist that present-day baseball is best. But I
know, and so does Bill Starr, that no one can *prove* when baseball
was at its best.

In an imaginary world, we could resurrect the best players
of the twenties and thirties, which would include Babe Ruth, Ty
Cobb, Tris Speaker, Bob Grove, Walter Johnson, Rogers Hornsby,
Lou Gehrig, et al, toss in Hans Wagner, Joe Jackson, and even
Christy Mathewson, have them form a 12-team league, and compete against a 12-team league made up of the best players from
1947 to today. They would play an interleague schedule only, head

to head. There would be a balancing of the changes in the game: the dead ball of the early years and the current-day livelier ball; in the size and shapes of the ball parks; artificial turf and natural grass; larger and smaller gloves; the batting helmet and the soft caps; the four-umpire and two-umpire systems; the different strike zones; the nonenforcement and the strict enforcement of the balk rule; daytime and nighttime baseball; traveling conditions; and so on. We'd have them go at it. I'll tell you something. When that season was over, it still wouldn't prove a thing.

What this book does certainly prove is that baseball—whether in the twenties, thirties, eighties, or nineties—is an incomparable game that will be discussed and read and argued about forever. Don't pass up this chance to add to your knowledge and enjoyment of the game, as chronicled by an expert who tells it like it is, and was.

—Ralph Kiner

INTRODUCTION

Looking back now, I can see that the seed for this book was planted in 1971, at a social event at Ralph Kiner's home in Rye, New York.

We were, not surprisingly, discussing baseball. Joining us was John K. Hutchens, a long-time member of the editorial staff of the Book-of-the-Month Club—and a triple-distilled, knowledgeable baseball enthusiast, as well. I was expounding on my long-held conviction that the best talent and the best baseball played was in the 1920s and 1930s. Kiner was equally insistent that the golden years in baseball were in the late 1940s and 1950s. He contended that the entrance of black and Latin players into the major leagues in those later years brought talent into the game that raised the quality of baseball to its greatest heights.

Kiner, ever the professional, challenged: "In what way was baseball better in the twenties and thirties? What skills did those players have that players don't have today?"

"It would take a book to answer those questions," I replied. It didn't occur to me that years later I would be involved in this undertaking as a response to Kiner's questions.

Although my recollections of the great players of the twenties and thirties gave me a perspective that Kiner didn't have, I realized that recollections alone are not proof. I also realized at that time that an open bar and a buffet table of food were beckoning me, which suddenly seemed more enticing than the pursuit of a discussion that had no possible resolution.

Before the evening was over, Kiner and I did connect on some points of agreement. We agreed that statistics were overrated as measurements of a player's true value. We agreed that the standard of major league baseball declined with the three expansions in the 1960s, from 16 teams to 24 (subsequently expanded to 26 teams in 1977). We touched upon the virtual destruction of the minor leagues in the early fifties, with no apparent relief in sight.

Those issues remained quiescent in me until 1983, when I was propelled into this book by a series of magazine articles that seemed to attack and demean the players of the twenties and thirties. To my amazement, the superstars, the Hall of Famers from those days, were the prime targets of these attacks.

The flashpoint was an article in an August 1983 issue of *Time* magazine, in which the claim was made that "there are any number of players today as good as anyone has ever been." Unbelievable! Does anyone seriously believe that "there are any number of players today" the equal of Babe Ruth, Ty Cobb, Tris Speaker, Rogers Hornsby, Eddie Collins, Charlie Gehringer, George Sisler, Lou Gehrig, Jimmie Foxx, Hank Greenberg, Al Simmons, Mel Ott, Gabby Hartnett, Bill Dickey, Walter Johnson, Bob Grove, Stan Musial, Joe DiMaggio, Ted Williams, and many other old-time Hall of Famers?

In quick succession, *Time* followed with an article quoting Pete Palmer—a nice man, but with an unfortunate dedication to the game of computerball, which attempts to define baseball strategies and the talents of players strictly by statistical analyses.

> [Palmer] thinks he can show that despite Hall of Famer [George] Sisler's career .340 average, he was clearly inferior as a batter to Norm Cash and Boog Powell, and only a bit better than the long-forgotten journeyman, Roy Sievers.

George Sisler in the journeyman class? Branch Rickey may claim that in all of his years in baseball, Honus Wagner was the greatest player he ever saw, with Sisler not far behind. But Rickey, the greatest judge of baseball talent and the most ingenious innovator in baseball's history, was apparently no match for an "expert" who has never played an inning of professional baseball or seen any of the great old-time players on the ball field.

Then followed a full-length book, *The Hidden Game of Baseball*, by John Thorn and Pete Palmer. Their book approximates a bible for their followers, the computerball statisticians. They cite another statistician, William D. Rubinstein, who published the following data in the 1981 *Baseball Research Journal*, under the auspices of the Society of American Baseball Research (SABR):

> If Ty Cobb's career had taken place . . . in 1976, his lifetime B.A. [batting average] would have been only .289. Rogers Hornsby and Joe DiMaggio [would] achieve identical .280 marks. Bill Terry, Lou Gehrig and Tris Speaker [would be] average to mediocre hitters at .271, .269 and .265 respectively. The Babe's .262 is a disappointment, though he hits better than Al Simmons' (.260) or Harry Heilmann's (.257); [or] Honus Wagner . . . "a good field no-hit" (.251). . . . On the other hand, today's players, even those who are not true superstars, would be veritable supermen in comparison . . . . Only Stan Musial's (.315), Roberto Clemente's (.313) . . . and Ted Williams' (.310) among the recent stars of the past really do well.

Dick Cramer, another SABR contributor, had done a study that provided a basis for Rubinstein's work. According to Thorn and Palmer, "Cramer employed an ingenious method of evaluating batting skill across time. He compared the batting performance of the same player in different seasons, avoiding the pitfall of environmental factors such as ball resistance, rule changes, racial mix, playing conditions, etc." What kind of meshugaas is that?

If these "experts" were correct in their conclusions about non-abilities of the Hall of Famers of the twenties, thirties, forties, and fifties, I could see my more than 65 years of studious observation of major league baseball go down the drain; my 20 years of direct professional experience would be a delusion; my memories of many of the great old-time players wrapped in nothing but sentiment and nostalgia.

The authors insist that their statistical analyses prove that the old-time Hall of Famers of the 1920s and 1930s were players of ordinary ability by today's standards. To them, these players were overrated, their records inflated and illusory. They single out Bill Terry, one of the greatest players in the history of baseball, as an example of mediocrity. I can visualize no scene more interesting than having these intrepid statisticians run their theories by old-timers such as Leo Durocher, Al Lopez, Bill Dickey, Luke Appling, Billy Herman, Charlie Gehringer, Bob Feller, Joe DiMaggio, and Ted Williams. These statisticians may know everything about computerized statistical analyses, but to the professionals in baseball, computerball statistics are bullshit!

This book is not intended as a Hot Stove League argument, evaluating and debating the records and talents of individual players, or teams, or leagues from one era to another. Such evaluations can never be proven, not by firsthand observations and especially not by statistics. Instead, the focus of this book is to provide some insights into the techniques, attitudes, and experiences of the players of the twenties and thirties; to show how they differed from current-day baseball; and to demonstrate Babe Ruth's impact on baseball, which raised the quality of the game to unprecedented heights.

To provide a clear picture of what baseball was like in the twenties and thirties requires the debunking of some of the myths and misconceptions that have cluttered its history; an understanding of the role of the minor leagues in the 1920s and 1930s; the views of the game as expressed by the old-time players and new-time managers who were interviewed for this book; and a familiarity with some of the fundamentals of baseball not generally appreciated by even the most dedicated fans.

This book does not rely upon statistics as decisive measurements of baseball talent. If a statistic is offered, it is peripheral to an issue—a sidelight, an incidental observation—with one major exception, the strikeout. Oddly, with all the obtuse statistics that the New Statisticians have conjured up in recent years, the strikeout, one of the most influential statistics of all, has been consistently overlooked, never understood, and therefore never evaluated.

Although baseball is presumed to be the national pastime, one of its most intriguing anomalies is that most fans do not really understand the game. In a sense baseball is two separate games. The fan sees the surface game; the professional views the subsurface. Watching a baseball game is analogous to looking at a painting. A casual observer sees the externals of a picture. An observer with a professional and more discerning eye sees the "inside" of the canvas, with its myriad technical details—brush strokes, shadings, form and composition—all of which provide greater meaning, more enlightened interest, and more enjoyment of the work.

These different perspectives, the view of the fan and that of the professional, have created a huge gulf of misunderstanding about baseball. Spanning this chasm becomes a necessity in order to bring the fans into the domain of the professionals, where they can acquire an understanding of the nuances and strategies of the game that have invariably eluded them. By observing baseball from the professionals' viewpoint, fans will obtain a more comprehensive, more critical, and more enjoyable understanding of what's happening on the ball field. Their judgments will never be wrong. No fan ever relinquishes the privilege of the second guess. Neither does the professional.

Paul Richards, a baseball luminary with over fifty years' experience as a player, manager, scout, and baseball executive, described baseball best with this quote in Donald Honig's book *The Men in the Dugout*: "Baseball's not made up of a few big plays and dramatic moments . . . but rather it's a beautifully put together pattern of countless little subtleties that add up to the big moments and you have to be very well versed in the game to fully appreciate it."

Not all the "moments" in baseball, as Paul Richards implies, are positive in nature. The negatives have an equal impact on the game, with poor fundamentals the principal contributor. For example, only an exceptional talent such as Johnny Bench could overcome the fundamentally unsound technique of one-handed catching. The rank and file of catchers who follow in Bench's wake fall far short of his talent. They really hurt their pitchers and their teams with the one-handed catching style.

How do we account for the proliferation of stolen bases in the game today? Conventional wisdom invariably places the onus of stolen bases on either the pitcher or the catcher—or on both of them. In many cases that's true. Yet, the infielders, including the first basemen, often make important contributions to the stolen base. Even the four-umpire system has made the stolen base a much cheaper commodity.

Before undertaking this book, I was beset with a nagging concern. How would I find the time and energy to interview old-time major leaguers who are scattered all over the country? Lawrence Ritter, in his wonderful book *The Glory of Their Times*, comments that his work in interviewing 22 old-timers consumed five years of his life and 75,000 miles of travel. At my age, I don't have five years to give to anyone. And 75,000 miles of travel presented an even more frightening prospect. Although I knew many of these old-time players from personal experience and was able to make direct contact with them, my concern was to reach those whom I did not know except by reputation. A pattern soon developed, however, that made such concerns academic. Players would break the ice for me by arranging contacts with other ex-major league players, through a phone call or by writing on my behalf. My discussions with the old-timers were not intended as oral histories. My interest was only on the style of their game, their experiences, their observations of their contemporaries, and their views of baseball today.

What may surprise many readers is the objectivity of the old-timers and their ready acknowledgment of the superior players in the game today, who would have been superior major-league players at any time in baseball. The attitude of the old-timers could best be described as professional detachment. That didn't surprise me. What all professionals in baseball admire most are the techniques and the productive skills of any player, regardless of the era or personality of the player. In my interviews, I did not find a single player who liked Ty Cobb as a person. Yet every one of them admired Ty Cobb's unique baseball talent.

Finally, as I put these words on paper I'm aware that I may be tampering with a flame that has never been extinguished in baseball's history—the subjectivity of the fans. Their attachments to certain teams and individual players are often lifetime affairs, sometimes handed down with undiminished fervor over the years, parent to child, not unlike a legacy. Thus, there is no intention here to tamper with devotions to favorite players and teams, nor to demean players of any era in the game. To become a major league player is to reach the highest level of efficiency in a most difficult game to play. Arguably, the most difficult of all.

What I've attempted, instead, is to provide an insight into baseball as it was played in the twenties and thirties. That was the time when the careers and livelihoods of its players were measured not in terms of long-term contracts, but on a month-to-month basis. It was a time when the annual payroll of an entire ball club was less than the salary of one average player today. It was a time when the game was played with a proficiency and intensity unsurpassed in any other era in baseball's history. Read on—and judge for yourself.

—Bill Starr
San Diego, February 1988

CLEARING THE BASES

1 After The Scandal

My long affair with baseball began in 1920, in a cinder-surfaced schoolyard in the Maxwell Street area of Chicago. From that time, my involvement with the game grew from curiosity to professional interest and over the years has evoked in me the gamut of emotions ranging from euphoria to despair.

On a particular September day in 1920, my little world was bombarded by the shouts of newsboys—*"Extra! Extra! Read all about it! White Sox players indicted!"* Those screams pierced the air with an intensity that seemed to exceed the excitement of the Armistice two years before.

The cries of the newsboys alarmed us. The word *indicted* had an ominous sound and a meaning that we kids did not understand. We'd heard the stories about the Sox players supposedly "throwing" the World Series with Cincinnati in the previous year. How could we possibly believe those yarns? We were ball players, too. We knew from our experiences in our schoolyard games the burning intensities in each of us to get a hit, to catch a ball, to score a run—to *win*. There *was* no other way to play the game, not for us and certainly not for our heroes, the gods of baseball, the American League Champions—the Chicago White Sox.

Yet none of this commotion disturbed our routines and our own brands of baseball. In the daytime it was softball. At night we improvised a game of baseball which we called peg and stick. The peg was a six-inch stub whittled out of a discarded broom handle. A two-foot length of the handle became the stick. A sharp rap by the stick propelled the peg from the ground into the air, and a whack put the "ball" in play, sending the batter scurrying around imaginary bases. The lighting system for our night games didn't exactly resemble the sophisticated installations in baseball today. We played under the shadowy luminescence of gas lights, with an opening ceremony provided by a lamplighter on horseback. Our ball fields were the dirt streets of our neighborhoods, where we competed for *Lebensraum* with hordes of peddlers. Our games were often interrupted by these purveyors with their braziers on wheels, hawking baked sweet potatoes, hot chick peas, and corn on the cob, whose tantalizing aromas linger in my consciousness to this day.

Actually that was only one-half of my world. The other part was the cheder, that staple of Orthodox Jewish schooling that tested the endurance, if not the faith, of a generation of Jewish youth. For me the cheder was two hours of daily agony that followed my attendance at the public grade school. The cheder of my days was ruled by an old-world rebbe, a martinet who guided the religious education of his unruly and mutinous charges through the influence of a weapon similar to a sawed-off cue stick. In later years, as a catcher in professional baseball, I was convinced that my manual dexterity derived from the skill I developed in avoiding the rebbe's attempts to use my knuckles for his batting practice.

Several weeks passed before the story of the scandal penetrated our consciousness. By that time the shocking news that eight White Sox players were charged with the crime of "throwing" the World Series reached every household and became *the* topic of conversation. The general reaction was—stunned disbelief.

Our sympathies were with the players. The enemy was Charles Comiskey, the White Sox owner. In retrospect, what a strange reversal of values. After all, it was not the owner but the players who betrayed the fans and created the scandal. But the fans and the press rationalized. They blamed Comiskey, stereotyped as a mean, ruthless, and tightfisted owner, for setting the stage for the crime. Eventually, a jury absolved the players. Their written confessions and other documents bearing on their guilt had somehow mysteriously disappeared, probably through Divine Providence, assisted by the hands of a friendly mortal or two.

Concurrently with their acquittal, however, came the decision from the new commissioner of baseball, Kenesaw Mountain Landis. He expressed the notion that players who conspired to take bribes for the purpose of rearranging the scores of baseball games were not performing precisely in the public interest. And so out they went, to be replaced in 1921 by virtually a new White Sox team.

At that time, although I was all of 10 years old, I assigned myself to the roster of the White Sox. The baseball bug had entered my bloodstream. I fantasized—*I knew*—that someday I would join that utopian existence, professional baseball.

My psychic escape route became baseball. During vacations, holidays, and even occasional truancies, my companions and I would make the trek to the White Sox park. Our usual mode of transportation was the tailgate of a truck or even a horse-drawn wagon. Occasionally, we did it the old-fashioned way, just hoofing it to 35th and Shields. Often we would arrive early enough to watch the special practices that were conducted long before the gates were opened.

As with all youngsters, we quickly created our heroes, who were not necessarily the superstar players. My favorite was not even a White Sox player. The player who won my greatest devotion was Billy Rogell, a young infielder with the Red Sox. As kids do today, after the games we would hang around outside the players' clubhouse to see them in street clothes, asking them whatever questions came to mind. I don't recall how it happened, but one afternoon following a game, I found myself walking alongside Rogell. He stopped at a vendor's cart to buy a hot dog and asked me, "Would you like one?" *Would I?* It must have been my lean and hungry look that prompted his invitation. Nothing has ever tasted better.

I understand that Rogell is a respected and admired individual in his community in Michigan, having served in political office among his other activities. For the price of a 10-cent hot dog Billy Rogell had won a lifelong admirer and a faithful, although non-voting, constituent.

The Sox' park was virtually my second home. When the Sox were on the road, I would, somewhat furtively, attend National League games at the Cubs' park, but not without guilt feelings for my infidelities to the Sox and the American League. But I managed to see them all, in both leagues, from the supergreat to the not-so-great.

In the 1920s, early morning practices were routine in the majors, even though the games were afternoon affairs. Those early practice sessions were independent of the customary pregame batting and fielding practices. I was fascinated with those workouts, which were almost entirely devoted to fundamentals. Among the kids on my block I soon felt that I was the authority on how the game was to be played.

In time, we began to recognize and emulate the styles of not only the White Sox players, but also players on other clubs. Even now I can recall the leisurely, preparatory swings of Harry Hooper, who would gracefully move his bat back and forth, like a pendulum, before finally resting it on his shoulder as he awaited the pitch. Or Eddie Collins, who would park his wad of gum on the button of his cap as he approached the plate. His straight-up batting stance, with his bat held in a perpendicular position, was similar to Ty Cobb, Harry Heilmann, George Burns, and many other exceptional hitters of those days.

We marveled at the skill of Johnny Mostil, the centerfielder for the White Sox, who played a shallow center field, as many center fielders did in those days. The ball was comparatively soft and lifeless then. On fly balls over his head, Mostil would turn his back to the infield and outrace the ball, stopping and turning at the precise spot to make the catch. Mostil was the defensive equal of Tris Speaker or any other center fielder who ever played the game. While researching for this book, I tried to track down the details of the story of Mostil catching a *foul* ball from his center field position. Bibb Falk, a teammate of Mostil, told me: "I heard about that catch, but it never happened while I was in the outfield. Mostil thought every fly ball anywhere in the outfield was his play. But I took care of my position without his help." Falk was a fixture in left field for the Sox, and at the time one of the best outfielders in the game. A Chicago paper once referred to him as an "exponent" of the diving catch, a word that fell into my vocabulary for the first time.

I asked Johnnie Kerr about Mostil's foul-ball catch. Kerr had been a teammate of his, and later a coach with Washington during my brief tenure on that club. "It happened," he said, "but not in a regular-season game. It was in spring training. Mostil was shaded to left center and a high fly got caught up in a strong wind. He kept chasing the ball until it reached foul territory. I don't remember who the left fielder was, but the outfielders always got out of the way when Mostil went after a ball. He was a very aggressive outfielder and a great one."

In the middle and late twenties, as a teenager, I began to participate in Sox practice sessions by offering my services as a batting practice catcher. I was given a threadbare, long-discarded uniform, which to me was like a mantle of gold. I asked for the assignment of catching batting practice because there is rarely a volunteer for that thankless job. It is absolutely the worst chore in baseball. Yet it had its compensations. I could see the players at close range and occasionally exchange a few words with them. The reward for my efforts was to grab a bat after the last player had his practice swings, and while fully garbed with a chest protector and shin guards, I would take a few swipes at the lobs of the batting practice pitcher.

The catching equipment that I wore was not exactly tailored for my frame. The chest protector dropped to a point below my knees. The shin guards were big enough to cover a part of my thighs. Yet my only problem was with a loose-fitting, oversized, two-bar mask. When a ball was fouled into it, this mask would go into an act of its own, bouncing a tattoo against my jaw, which always came out second best in this one-sided battle. And, as a moth to the flame, I would return for more punishment. Catching equipment is truly the tools of ignorance.

My exposure to major league baseball in the 1920s had the effect of making me more of a serious student than a fan. Thus, when I began my minor-league playing career in 1931, I had a built-in interest in observing and gauging the talents of players. My nine-year career as a player was almost entirely in the minor leagues, with a short stay with Washington in 1935 and 1936. Players who manage a few games in the majors are said to have had "a cup of coffee" in that select company. With me it was more of a demitasse.

It didn't take long for me to learn a fact that was indigenous to major league baseball during that time. If you wore a major league uniform—even if you were a rookie freshly arrived from Harrisburg of the class-A New York–Penn League—you were expected to know the fundamentals of baseball.

Within a day or two of my joining Washington in 1935, I was inserted into the lineup in the ninth inning of a game in Chicago. We had a one-run lead. After two outs, Chicago got two runners on base and I got a dilemma. Radcliff was on first and Al Simmons on third—a perfect setup for a double steal with a rookie catcher behind the plate.

What do I do if Radcliff breaks for second? Do I throw to second and chance Simmons breaking for home and scoring the tying run? Will Buddy Myer, our second baseman, cut off my throw and return it to me? The chances are real that my first throw in the major leagues will end up in center field. Surely Jimmie Dykes, the Chicago manager, must know my problem. He's certain to start the double steal. Do I fake a throw to second and try to trap Simmons off third?

This bothers me. If Simmons doesn't take the bait, I would permit the potential winning run to get into scoring position. That would be a cardinal violation of good baseball.

I could have used some help. Yet no manager, coach, or player approached me, offering a word of advice. It would have been demeaning for me to ask for help. My uniform had Washington on it. That made me a major league player. I was supposed to know how to handle this situation.

I decided—To hell with it! I'm throwing through to second. If Simmons, a brute of a man, comes barreling home, I'll put my one-hundred-seventy-pound frame in front of the plate. I might be propelled into the backstop screen, with my glove, the ball, and other catching equipment scattered over the premises, but I'm biting the bullet.

Much to my relief, nothing that dramatic happened. Jack Russell, our pitcher, threw the next pitch, the batter lofted a lazy fly to center, and the game was over. All my heavy-duty thinking went down the drain, but the lesson was learned. Players were supposed to know the fundamentals of baseball when reaching the major leagues. At least that's how it was in those days. I also learned that Dykes would never rank as a manager with such as Leo Durocher, Bucky Harris, Lefty O'Doul, or the many astute managers of modern times.

I was sold to San Diego in 1937. Ted Williams was on that club at the time, and I had the unique experience of pinch-hitting for him. In candor, it was a fluke.

As with all great hitters, Williams was never called upon to bunt. As with all ordinary hitters, I was often asked to bunt. We were in a tie game with Seattle. We had a man on first with nobody out in the last of the ninth, Ted Williams at bat, facing a right-handed pitcher. Our manager, Frank Shellenback, had Williams swinging, and he hit a foul—strike one. Shellenback then pulled Williams and sent me to the plate to bunt the runner to second. I bunted a foul—strike two—and then flied out. In later years I located the story of the game, which carried an asterisk at the bottom of the box score: "*Starr batted for Williams." This furnished me with a ready response to my friends, who often needled me about my ineffectiveness as a hitter: "I was good enough to pinch-hit for Ted Williams."

My playing career ended in 1939 in San Diego, where I settled and entered the business world. In 1944 I formed a syndicate that purchased the Pacific Coast League franchise of the San Diego Padres. I became the principal owner and its chief executive for 11 years thereafter. As an independent club, we were able to compete for talent with the majors—perhaps at a disadvantage but, nevertheless, with some degree of success. We had our own farm system, employed part-time scouts, and developed many players for sale to the majors, which provided us not only with needed cash, but also with players as part of the transactions. After the 1955 season I sold my interests in the Padres and retired from baseball ownership.

With my 20-year involvement in professional baseball at an end, I resigned myself to the status of a fan. From the confines of the stands, I am now able to make my baseball judgments with never a mistake, although admittedly sometimes after the fact. Even to this day my special interest in baseball is geared to appraising baseball talent and the quality of play.

Having watched major league baseball for these many years, I have yet to see a higher standard of play than that of the twenties and thirties. In discussing baseball, every old-timer has to contend with the allegations that nostalgia has replaced his good judgment, or even his senses, and that his objectivity has gone out the window. These charges never sit well. It is the rare professional who doesn't appreciate talent wherever and whenever he sees it.

Recently, I came across some quotes of mine in an interview with a San Diego sports writer in 1970. I was not indulging in nostalgia then, nor am I now. I stated:

> Baseball players are not better today than they were 20 years ago, or even 40 years ago. The size-strength ratio that is used for basketball and football athletes cannot be used for baseball. Baseball players don't rely on strength and size. It's more a matter of reflexes. . . . Today there is an appalling lack of good hitters. I'm always surprised when I read that some star player believes he's had a great year by hitting .280 with 25 home runs and 80 to 90 runs batted in, even though he's struck out 125 to 150 times. . . . Among present-day major leaguers, Pete Rose is one player who plays the game the way it was years ago. He rarely strikes out, he swings with half a bat, hits .300, gets 200 hits a year and makes $100,000.

The only change I would make today in that article, would be to add another zero to Rose's subsequent salary as a player. Otherwise, my convictions are the same as before.

In my interviews with many old-timers, whose views are an integral part of this book, I didn't encounter a single one who wasn't impartial in his appraisals of current-day players and how the game is played today. They might be outspoken and critical when comparing conditions between their era and current days. Or when discussing the modern-day players' preoccupation with their own statistics. Or when commenting on the foolishness of computerized statistical analyses that presume to pass authoritative judgment on the talents of players, generation by generation. But the old-timers I talked to were not motivated by nostalgia. Neither am I.

2 Faster, Bigger, Stronger— FBS, as in FIBS

"It does violence to common sense to suppose that while athletes in every other sport today are measurably and vastly superior to those 50 to 75 years ago, in baseball alone the quality of play is stagnant or in decline."

—The Hidden Game of Baseball,
by *Thorn and Palmer*

Myths cling to the fabric of baseball as barnacles to a ship, harmless excrescences that go with the territory. They provide anecdotal material to feed the insatiable appetites of fans, but unfortunately some myths distort important aspects of the game. Through the alchemy of repetition, baseball historians, sports writers, and especially the new breed of statisticians have managed to endow these distortions with a specious validity, transmuting them into unshakable "truths." These myths must be excised if we are to understand the realities of the game.

Probably the most obvious development in all sports over the years has been the progression in the size, strength, and speed of its athletes. In no sport is this more apparent than in football or basketball, where super physical specimens dominate. Size, strength, and speed are prerequisites for participating in those sports today. No argument there. What is basic for football and basketball, however, is not always applicable to baseball. A knee-jerk reaction has set in with the media and the statisticians, who automatically bracket baseball with the other two sports. If football and basketball are better today, then so must it be for baseball. That conclusion is not valid. It is surprising that, to my knowledge, not a single sports writer has undertaken to challenge that specious reasoning.

Baseball does not belong in a trinity with football and basketball. True, these three sports share many common characteristics: They are the major professional spectator sports in the country, through direct attendance or by television viewing. All operate under the control of commissioners. They have similarities in preseason training, scheduling, playoffs, and championship games. They recruit talent much in the same way, through player drafts, trades, and free agencies. For better or worse, they are in a continuous state of combat over compensation, which on occasion results in a strike. But beyond these surface features, baseball is entirely different from football and basketball.

Baseball has a greater kinship to golf, which does not require excessive size or strength for its participants. Both of these games are played with hand tools. In baseball, with its ball and glove, it is the skill with which the players use their hand tools—their implements—that determines the value of the players.

The key to hitting the long ball in baseball is the same as in golf—maximum club-head speed at the point of impact. Every member of every golf course can single out a 130- or 140-pound golfer who can drive a ball longer distances than golfers of far more imposing size and strength. There are women golfers who can outdrive men. In baseball, as in golf, the long-ball hitters include little guys as well as bigger and stronger specimens. Freddie Patek, a shortstop who played for the California Angels, hit three home runs in a game against the Boston Red Sox in June of 1980. Patek stood five feet five inches and weighed 148 pounds.

The history of baseball is replete with small-sized players who could hit the long ball. Of course, bigger and stronger players will often hit longer balls. But hitting a ball 5 or 10 or 15 rows farther into the stands brings no greater reward than a ball that just clears the wall. They are all the same in the box score. Baseball is a game for all sizes.

As the old song goes, "It don't mean a thing if you ain't got that swing." San Diego Padres announcer Jerry Coleman, a former New York Yankees infielder, commented: "One of the strongest guys I ever met in baseball was Bill Renna. He was about six foot three, weighed about 225 pounds—all muscle. But he couldn't get the bat around. Little guys like Nellie Fox or Billy Goodman had more snap in their swings." Whitey Herzog of the Cardinals explained his disposal of Ken Oberkfell: "He's as big and strong as Mantle, but all he does is hit singles to the opposite field." In baseball, it doesn't matter how much faster, bigger, and stronger a player may become. Those attributes are of no help to a player with poor reflexes and a slow bat.

An example was Hack Wilson, who led the National League with 56 home runs in 1930 and set a National League record with 190 RBIs. I was on the same ball club with Wilson, in Albany of the International League in 1935, when his days as a major leaguer were over. The best he could do with Albany was 3 home runs in 59 games. He still possessed physical strength, but waning reflexes brought his career to an end.

I recall an ironic experience with Hack Wilson, who was my roommate on the Albany club. In those days, the practice was to pair players in accordance with the management's idea of players with opposite moral habits. I assume that Wilson was considered the rowdy and that I, as an offshoot from a rabbinical family, was to be the leavening influence on him.

On one road trip I went out with a couple of the other players for a night on the town. It was past midnight when I returned to our hotel. I couldn't find my room key. I pounded on the door and woke up a sleepy and grouchy Hack Wilson. He grumbled at me, "Why in hell don't you try to get to bed on time?" And

I was the guy who was supposed to be his watchdog. What is it they say about "the best laid plans of mice and men"?

He told me a remarkable story involving the 56 home runs he hit for the Cubs in 1930. The Elgin Watch Company had a deal with Hack to give him a certificate, good for one Elgin watch, for each home run he hit that year. Certificates were sent to him after each home run, a total of 56:

> My pockets seemed to be stuffed with these pieces of paper. I'd walk down the street and some fan would stop me and tell me how nice it would be if I could hit a home run for his son or grandson. What they wanted was an Elgin certificate. This happened wherever I went. Pretty soon I was handing out certificates with every request. At the end of the season, my wife phones me from Virginia to tell me she's coming to Chicago and that we will go to the Elgin Company and trade in my 56 certificates for a diamond watch for her. I didn't have one certificate left over. So I laid out $2,500 in cash to buy her a watch.

Although Hack no longer had the talent of his great years with the Chicago Cubs, he still had the demeanor and charisma of a star. He was generous to a fault. On a trip to Montreal, Hack invited me to go along with him, following our afternoon game. I accepted, of course. Soon we were at a long bar in a pub where other players were assembled. No one was allowed to buy a drink as long as Wilson was in the party. His style was to place a wad of money on one end of the bar, instructing the bartender to "set 'em up for the boys" until all the money was gone. Unfortunately, his reflexes with the bat didn't match his facility for picking up bar checks and doling out gift certificates.

Body size and muscular development are no guarantees of power hitting or of overriding skill in any sport that requires the use of implements. Baseball players may continue to become better physical specimens as their natural growth and their training methods continue to improve, as it has over the past 50 years or more. But successful results on the ball field will still depend more upon their dexterity with the tools of their trade—the bat, the glove, and the ball—plus that special attribute, their quickness.

Quickness in baseball is characterized by short, swift, reflexive movements of a player, whether by the snap of his bat while hitting or in his actions on defense. Speed is an advantage and great speed is a greater advantage, but quickness comes into play more often than blazing speed.

The pitcher who can glove a hard-hit ball before it zips through the box into centerfield for a hit, is quick. The infielder who can turn a double play before being upended by a hard-sliding runner, is quick. Sheer foot speed is not enough. For an infielder, what counts are nimble feet, a quick release of the ball, and the agility to evade sliding base runners. For example, no one has ever claimed that Bill Mazeroski, an exceptionally gifted second baseman for Pittsburgh from 1956 to 1972, was blessed with even average running speed. Twenty-seven stolen bases in a 17-year career indicates his fleetness of foot. Yet if a rating were compiled of second basemen who were quick and proficient in executing the double play, Mazeroski's name would be high on the list.

Mental alertness is certainly a component of quickness, as are sharp reflexes. These are basic needs for the successful major league player. Of course, these intangibles combined with super-lative physical talent produce that rarity—the superstar player.

Ozzie Smith, the St. Louis Cardinals' shortstop, is an example of the many players in the game today who are not exceptional physical specimens but are superior players nonetheless. Smith's greatness stems from his quickness, in combination with the special physical attributes of "soft" hands and acrobatic agility. These extraordinary gifts earn Smith the reputation as probably the best defensive shortstop ever to play the game and the distinction of being among the highest-paid players in baseball.

The basic physical needs for a successful major league player are the ability to hit the ball with precise timing, to field the ball skillfully, to throw the ball hard and accurately, and of course, a reasonable degree of foot speed. These requirements are not the automatic products of exceptional muscular development and strength.

To throw a ball "hard" or for great distances is not exclusive with the big and the strong. "Bullet" Joe Bush, Tommy Bridges, Bobby Shantz, Billy Pierce, Ron Guidry, Camilo Pascual, and Ted Higuera are but a few of the many smaller guys who rank with the hard-throwing pitchers in baseball's history. If put to a test, a 250-pound football behemoth or a seven-foot basketball giant could not throw a baseball farther than many baseball players 100 pounds lighter and a foot shorter. Even oversized baseball players often have weaker throwing arms than much smaller players.

The bulk and body fat that football players are programmed to acquire would be fatal to the career of a major league baseball player. A height of seven feet may be prized in basketball, but in baseball such excessive size would be a liability. There are many instances of athletes who are college trained in all three professional sports, football, basketball, and baseball. They are often the possessors of superb, well-developed bodies, and invariably, the one sport that they are unable to master is baseball—major league and even minor league variety.

Yet, the FBS theory persists. One writer expresses this theory with this astonishing opinion: "If a host of new track and field Olympic records established every year are any indication, they can run faster and farther, why shouldn't they bat better?"

Someday, among all its other citations, the Hall of Fame may reserve a section for the most egregious non sequiturs ever expressed in baseball. The above statement is sure to be a first–ballot winner. Joe Garagiola at his best couldn't match that one.

It is the failure to recognize baseball's particular requirements that has thrown the media and the statisticians off the track. In the 1960s, Leonard Koppett, a prominent baseball writer, also fell victim to these misconceptions in his book *All about Baseball.* He wrote:

> Older players and older fans will often give the simplest answer: the players aren't as good as they were in the old days; nobody knows how to hit; the art has been lost. This explanation can be dismissed as more simpleminded than simple, and as just plain silly. *Athletes have improved in every measurable respect and they have improved in baseball, too.* [The emphasis is added to stress another example of the FBS theory at work.]

Granted that players today may be faster, bigger, and stronger. The "simple" question is: Does that automatically make them better players? The not so "silly" answer is: Baseball talent and quality of play are not strictly dependent upon the physical measurements of the players.

If one is to accept the reasoning that baseball players become more skilled year after year as they become faster, bigger, and stronger, the presumption must hold that players who started their careers around the turn of the century were virtually talentless by today's standards. If so, what do we make of Branch Rickey's claim that Honus Wagner was the greatest player he ever saw? What do we do with players such as Christy Mathewson, Cy Young, Nap Lajoie, Ed Walsh, Sam Crawford, Ty Cobb, Eddie Collins, Rogers Hornsby, George Sisler, Walter Johnson, Tris Speaker, Zack Wheat, and hundreds of others who excelled before, during, and after the twenties? And how do we explain a certain player named Babe Ruth, who began his career in 1914?

In the early 1960s—in his book, *The American Diamond*—Branch Rickey tried to come to grips with this issue. Rickey made his point, in part, by the use of home run statistics. He compared the home runs hit in the American League in 1927 with the home runs hit in 1961. He selected the 10 leading home-run hitters in the American League in 1927 and 1961, excluding Babe Ruth, Lou Gehrig, Mickey Mantle, and Roger Maris. He established that the average for those 10 hitters was 12.4 home runs per player in 1927, against an average of 34.1 home runs in 1961.

"Is it credible," he asked, "that within the span of time from 1927 to 1961 . . . young men have increased their power threefold? If so, it is credible that in another 24 years it would bring us to a team of supermen, with every man a mythical Hercules."

Rickey didn't make clear why he selected 24 years after 1961, the year of 1985, for baseball to greet the arrival of teams of supermen. Have the post-1961 years really produced superman results? If the home run is a symbol of greatness, the chart below may provide some answers to Rickey's questions. The chart lists the home runs achieved by the combined leagues over 10-year cycles from 1920, with adjustments made to establish a constant of 16 teams playing a 154-game schedule.

AVERAGE HOME RUN COUNT—BOTH LEAGUES

10-Year Cycles	Per Team Per Year
1920–29	62
1930–39	84
1940–49	81
1950–59	130
1960–69*	127
1970–79*	117
1980–87† (7-year cycle)	129

*Adjusted to 16 teams, 154-game schedule.
†1981 strike year excluded.

What does this chart prove? Nothing—except that there has been no consistent upward trend in home run hitting to support the FBS theory. If size and strength are the basic necessities for achieving home run power, then it must follow that ball players have been on a physical roller coaster since 1920.

How do we account for the limited number of home runs from 1920 through 1939, supposedly the era of the lively ball? The home run statistics for this 20-year period are distorted and deceiving. The players responsible for the distortions were Babe Ruth and Lou Gehrig.

For example, in the 10-year span, 1925 through 1934, Ruth and Gehrig hit more than half of all the home runs hit by their Yankee team. Although Ruth and Gehrig were superb physical specimens, they were not stronger than the other players on their club. Certainly not twice as strong. Further, during the 20-year cycle from 1920 through 1939, the Yankees averaged 139 home runs per year. Yet the remaining 15 major league teams hit only 69 home runs per team, half as many as the Yankees. Applying the faster, bigger, and stronger theory, does this prove that the players on all the other clubs were lesser physical specimens then the Yankees? Or that the players from Babe Ruth's time ran the gamut of physical weaklings to spectacular supermen?

Players may be faster, bigger, and stronger today than in previous years. And they may continue to increase their physical measurements in the years ahead. But such growth does not yield a concurrent increase in power hitting and home runs. Of greater importance are the more prosaic changes in baseball, such as the manufacture of increasingly resilient baseballs and the construction of ball parks whose dimensions are tailored for the production of home runs. The introduction of fences in front of the original outfield walls is now a common sight in baseball. They make home runs achievable for even the weakest hitters. Never in the history of baseball has it been easier to hit home runs than it is today. The idea that the quality of baseball automatically improves with each passing year because of the physical growth of its players is a myth that should be given final interment, once and for all.

3 | The Myth of the Lively Ball

"Never get into an argument with people who buy ink by the barrel."
—from the collected apothegms
of Satchel Paige, philosopher

Despite Satchel's admonition, there is a compelling need to stem the tide of media misinformation about one of the most tenacious canards in baseball, the so-called "lively ball" of the twenties and thirties. No single factor has distorted the perception of baseball as played in those days more than this deplorable myth. It has become the basis on which the New Statisticians concoct their comparisons of the talents of players from different eras—with the players of the 1920s and 1930s always getting the worst of it.

The lively ball appears as "fact" in every baseball encyclopedia and publication, and in every analysis of the game by sports writers, commentators, and statisticians. The prevailing supposition is that the ball was juiced up in 1920 to satisfy the demands of the fans for more long-ball hitting, especially for Babe Ruth—and not incidentally, to deflect "the glare" of the 1919 World Series scandal.

The Baseball Encyclopedia (Macmillan) claims that in 1920, in order to

> take advantage of the rising popularity of a young star named Babe Ruth, *the ball was made much livelier.* . . . This combination of Ruth, *the lively ball,* and the publicity generated by the New York City press took much of *the glare of attention away from the scandal of the 1919 World Series.* . . .[Emphasis added.]

The Sports Encyclopedia (Grosset & Dunlap) states that in 1920, "*aided by a livelier ball,* Ruth hit 54 home runs in this first season in New York." [Emphasis added.]

The Official Encyclopedia of Baseball (Turkin and Thompson) states: "Recognizing the gate attraction of the Bambino's homeric slams, the magnates quickly agreed to introduce the lively ball."

Robert W. Creamer, in his fine book *Babe*, says that in 1920 they ". . . pepped up the ball. No hard irrefutable facts exist to verify this—indeed, a laboratory test in August 1920 'proved' the ball had not been changed—but . . . [there seemed to be] overwhelming circumstantial evidence."

In fairness, the resiliency of the baseball was a small and peripheral part of Mr. Creamer's story on Babe Ruth. He is correct that "no hard irrefutable facts exist to verify" a lively ball. He is incorrect that "there seemed to be overwhelming circumstantial evidence" in support of the fiction that a special lively ball was introduced in 1920.

On the contrary, there is hard evidence, as well as circumstantial evidence, that no changes were made in the design, specifications, or construction of the baseball from 1910, when the cork center baseball was introduced, until 1931, when a thin cushion of cork and rubber was applied to the outside of the center core. The records in Cooperstown, the minutes of major league meetings, and numerous independent tests and experiments by experts all corroborate the fact that the resiliency of the baseball was not changed in 1920—not for Babe Ruth or for any other purpose. But the most compelling evidence are the experiences of the old-time players themselves. Without exception, they are clear and emphatic that the baseball used during their careers was "soft" and "dead." Obviously a soft and dead baseball cannot be lively, too.

Although 1920 was a turning point for baseball, it had nothing to do with a rejuvenated ball. It indeed had everything to do with the most remarkable player in baseball's history—Babe Ruth. But he did not save baseball, as it is suggested, by deflecting "the glare" of the scandal. Babe Ruth's achievements in 1919 and 1920 predated the discovery of the scandal, which did not surface until the end of the 1920 season. If the game needed saving, any credit for its redemption should go to Judge Landis, who became baseball's first commissioner in 1919. His stern magisterial demeanor, his reputation as a tough, uncompromising federal judge, and his immediate decision to expel the perpetrators of the "Black Sox" scandal virtually ensured baseball's integrity and stability.

The year 1920 was a watershed year for baseball that sent the pre-1920 style of hitting into oblivion. To the historians, it was baseball's equivalent of the Continental Divide; the years prior to 1920 were labeled the "dead-ball era," and the twenties and thirties designated as "the era of the lively ball." Both labels are misnomers. More accurate terminology would be "the pre-Ruthian" and "the Ruthian" eras.

To better understand the fallacy of the lively-ball theory, it is necessary to get a glimpse of baseball prior to the twenties, the dead-ball, pre-Ruthian years. By current-day standards, home run hitting was comparatively nonexistent then. This was not due only to an inherently dead baseball. The major cause was the ball parks with their distant fences, as much as 450 feet down the foul lines and over 500 feet to center field. An over-the-fence home run was a virtual impossibility. The distant fences of those ball parks shaped the style of the game and dictated the design of the bat. In fact, the evolution of baseball can be traced to the evolution of the ball parks and to the changes in the weight and shape of the bat.

There was logic and prudent economics in the huge distances of those early-day parks. Unlike ball parks today, which are con structed and owned by their municipalities, the parks of the pre-Ruthian era were privately owned. Money was always in short supply. Why tie up hard-pressed funds in outfield seating that would not be used except on a few special occasions? Capacity crowds did not occur often. On those special occasions any over-flow could be channeled to the outfield with plenty of standing room for everybody.

The outfield crowds were a mixed blessing that worked for and against the hitters. Normally, a drive between the outfielders was at least a triple. With crowds in the outfield, such hits were limited to ground rule doubles. Fly balls that were easily catchable under ordinary circumstances would often land in the crowd, a gift two-base hit for the batter.

The long ball of the pre-Ruthian years, the most exciting hit of its times (as it is today), was the inside-the-park home run, with the three-base hit not far behind. Those spectacular hits were the products of the oversized parks.

Tommy Leach was all of five feet six inches in height, weighing 150 pounds. To current-day fans it seems incongruous that anyone of not more than Little League size could ever lead a major league with six home runs, as Leach did in 1902. His homers, of course, were all inside the park.

Even more astonishing, in 1912, Owen Wilson, a Pittsburgh player, hit 36 triples. This outstanding feat almost defies belief. The smaller and enclosed parks of today lend themselves more readily to home runs than to triples. Leach's six inside-the-park home runs would be a rarity today, and 36 triples are even more improbable. Thus, under the ballpark conditions of those early days, with the excessive distances to the outfield fences, the style of the game and the type of bat that was used made considerable sense.

The bat, like the tools or implements of any other trade, was designed to suit a particular job. There was no need for a bat that would propel long fly balls that could easily be run down by the outfielders and converted into long outs. Line drives were the ideal and could best be accomplished by climbing up on the bat handle and applying the fat end of the bat to the ball with a flat, even swing.

Line-drive hitting required a thick-handled bat that provided "good wood" wherever it made contact with the ball. Many followers of baseball have seen pictures of the bat used before the 1920s. It had no recognizable barrel end, unlike the modern bat. It had a minimum of tapering, giving the impression that it could be swung with almost equal effectiveness from either end. If the modern-day player could be put into a time warp and sent backward into the early years of baseball, he would use exactly the same type of bat and play the same style of game as the old-timers did.

In 1910 a seemingly innocuous alteration in the composition of the baseball became the forerunner of a series of events that bedeviled baseball for the next 10 years. This involved mixing a portion of cork into the rubber core of the ball, creating the "cork center" baseball. The intent was to provide a bit more liveliness to the ball. This resulted in a commotion all out of proportion to its significance.

From the turn of the century, a de facto condition prevailed that permitted pitchers to employ illegal pitches, such as the spitball, with no quibbling from any quarter. The cork-center ball, however, evidently disturbed the pitchers of that time, and they countered with an assault on the baseball as if it was their mortal enemy. The spitball now became a standard weapon. In addition to the spitter, there was a proliferation of mud balls, emery and shine balls, with pitchers on every team getting into the act, using one or more of these specialties. Nothing became more unusual than the common fastball. The ball was routinely scuffed, and it was often cut with a prong that was attached to a belt buckle, or with a ring, or with a metal projection in the strap of the glove. On crucial occasions, pitchers were known to insert a pin into the stitching of the ball, as if applying the "coup de grace" to the hapless object. It was open season on the defenseless baseball, with no limit to the frustrations of the hitters.

The most accomplished of the practitioners of these creative pitching techniques were Hod Eller, Eddie Cicotte, and Russ Ford, with disciples on every team. Yet no one was more ingenious than Russ Ford, the originator of the emery ball. By concealing a piece of emery paper in his glove and cutting an opening in the pocket, he was able to rough up the cover of the ball. This produced some startling effects. The ball would sink, sail, or dance its way to the plate, often taking off in directions that baffled even the pitcher and catcher. Under ordinary circumstances a hitter could prepare himself at the plate, secure in the knowledge that the ball would move in a predictable direction. But how does one come to grips with a "doctored" pitch that dips sharply downward or sails at the last split second, or with a baseball that is so discolored as to create a multi-toned effect on its path to the plate? One is tempted to award Russell Ford a special, belated tribute for his ingenuity.

Throughout the teens, the proliferation of illegal pitches was a source of acute distress to Ban Johnson and John Heydler, presidents of the American League and National League, respectively. Accordingly, at the end of the 1919 season, the owners were persuaded to adopt measures to put an end, once and for all, to all illegal pitches. There would be no more "doctoring" of the baseball.

Thus, in 1920, all the freak pitches were abolished—excepting the spitball, which was given a one-year stay of execution. In all,

17 pitchers, whose livelihoods depended upon the spitter, were sanctioned to use it in 1920 only. No more than 2 spitball pitchers were permitted on any one club. This reprieve was subsequently extended to 1923, by which time, thanks to attrition, only 5 spitball pitchers remained, Burleigh Grimes, Red Faber, Urban Shocker, John Quinn, and Clarence Mitchell.

The other freak-ball pitchers were known and carefully watched. Anyone who brought the ball or the glove to his mouth, besides a sanctioned spitball pitcher, faced immediate removal from the game and an automatic fine. In those days, fines were not paid by the ball clubs. They were extracted directly out of the pitchers' meager earnings, an intolerable condition for them. The pitchers' travail became the hitters' delight.

In 1920, in addition to the abolition of the "freak" pitches, the pitchers were further handicapped by the slickness of the baseball. The manufacturers buried the stitches in the ball by undercutting the openings in the cover. The pitchers found it more difficult to grip the ball, which, in turn, reduced the effectiveness of their "breaking" pitches.

Yet none of these pitching handicaps made the impact on hitting as much as the influence of Babe Ruth. It is impossible to exaggerate his effect upon the media, the fans, and the game itself. Babe Ruth influenced baseball to a degree never matched by any player in its history. He established that hitting was the name of the game, the commodity that generated more fan enthusiasm, more gate receipts, and the basis for more money in the players' paychecks. The dramatic increase in fan interest produced a need for more seating, resulting in the construction of permanent outfield stands, which, in turn, shortened the distances and made home runs more achievable.

Concurrently, the shape of the bat and batting styles began to change. The Ruth type of bat, with its thinner handle and barrel end, became the new model for most of the players. In 1920, batting averages began to climb, reaching a peak in 1930. Years later, Branch Rickey commented: "Babe Ruth changed the whole objective in hitting. He not only changed modern-day baseball with his home run hitting, he also influenced bat design."

Jigger Statz, one of the great center fielders of the game, told of joining the New York Giants in 1919 out of Holy Cross University and playing 21 games as a replacement for the injured Ross Youngs. He said:

> It wasn't the baseball that changed. It was the bat and the batting styles. And Babe Ruth was responsible for all of it. In those days, the standard was a heavy, thick-handled bat. We choked up on the handle so as to get the fat end on the ball. Our swings were level, geared for line drives, not long balls. In 1920, in spring training and in batting practice before games, our players began to experiment with lighter bats, swinging from the end and trying for the long ball. We began to drop balls into the stands. Players began to make changes in their batting strokes. They were especially interested in the money Ruth was making. Major league players don't easily change their batting styles. But Babe Ruth made believers of us. The changes were gradual, but it began to pick up momentum with all the other major league clubs. Even I hit 10 home runs for the Cubs in 1923. In my previous years I totaled exactly 1.

No player of Ruth's time or since, has been able to influence the outcome of a game as he did. Jimmie Reese, now a coach with the California Angels, has been in professional baseball since 1921, and was a roommate of Babe Ruth with the Yankees in 1931 and 1932. He commented:

> In my 67 years in baseball, I've never seen a player as dominant on a ball club as Babe Ruth. And we had some pretty good players on the Yankees when I was with them. The veteran players on the club were always talking about the Babe's clutch hitting, his ability to rise to the occasion with a dramatic home run when most needed. In those

days, if a game went into extra innings there was the likelihood of the game being postponed because of darkness, or sometimes to meet a train schedule. Time after time, the Babe would break up a game with a last-time-at-bat home run. He loved those dramatic situations.

I recall one extra-inning game: The Babe was picking up his bat for his last time in the game, before postponement. I called out to him, "Bet you 10 dollars you can't hit one out of here." He called back, "You're on." Sure enough, he hit one out of the park. As he rounded third base, he hollered, "Reese, you owe me 10 bucks." I was happy to pay him. The next day he treated me to one of the greatest dinners in my life.

During the 1920s, when I was a denizen of the White Sox' park, I was often privileged to see Babe Ruth in action, in batting practice and during games. In the spring of 1935 I had an even better look at the Babe. At that time, I was in spring training with Albany of the International League. We were playing an exhibition game one day, with the Braves, who had Babe Ruth on their club. I was catching for Albany, and as the Babe approached the plate, I couldn't resist greeting him: "How are you, Babe—feeling OK?"

He nodded and responded, "Yeah, pretty good."

I then passed on some information, as catchers occasionally do for favorite players. "We'll be throwing you fastballs today, Babe. Nothing fancy." I wanted him to slug the ball.

Babe Ruth's stance at the plate was different from any other player I ever saw. Many hitters have closed stances, with their front foot diagonal to their back foot. Babe Ruth did more than that. He had his right shoulder turned in, almost pointing at me.

The first pitch we threw him was a fastball "away." To this day I've never seen a ball hit like that one. He seemed to make contact almost two feet before the ball reached the plate. With just a flick of his wrists he sent the ball off like a rifle shot, banging it against the left-center tin wall in our park. He ambled to second base for a double. His next time at bat, I called for the same pitch, with same result: another line drive resounded off the left-center metal fence.

Ruth was playing first base for the Braves that day. In one of the later innings Hack Wilson, one of our Albany outfielders, hit a ground ball to the infield. The throw to the Babe was off line, toward the inside of the bag. As Ruth came off the base to take the throw, Wilson crashed into him. Both players went down. There on the ground, in a tangled heap, lay the two greatest home-run hitters of their time. There was much concern whether either of them could stand up. Eventually they did, each with a damaged leg. Holding on to each other, they hobbled off the field to the dugout, possessing but two good legs between them.

Ruth's home runs in the early twenties not only shook up the fans and the press, but they had an even greater effect on the players. He brought the focus of the players' attention to the money end of the bat. In 1920, player salaries were measured in hundreds of dollars a month, for Babe Ruth it was in the thousands. It was evident that home runs and money were not only kindred spirits but were firmly bound to each other. For the players of the twenties and thirties, home runs meant money. The long ball was equated with an addition to a house, acres of farmland, hunting equipment, and a variety of acquisitions that only extra money could produce.

Despite the box office windfalls that the owners were enjoying in the advent of the Ruthian era, they were nervous and defensive over the burgeoning batting averages. Many of them were still rooted in an earlier time when the home run was a rarity, and when high batting averages were limited to a few superstars. Suspicions began to surface. The press was claiming that the owners had inserted a souped-up baseball into the game to further excite the fans—and not coincidentally, to inflate gate receipts. The owners were challenged to prove otherwise.

On June 20, 1920, *The New York Times* reported on a major league meeting with Thomas Shibe, a member of the firm that manufactured all the balls used in the American League. Mr. Shibe was also the vice president of the Philadelphia Athletics. The article quoted Mr. Shibe:

> The baseball used this year is the same as used last year and several seasons before that. The specifications call for the same yarn, the same cork center, the same size and weight and the same horsehide. It has not been changed one iota and no effort has been made to make the ball livelier. . . . With all the freak deliveries dead and the spitter almost dead, batters are able to hit the ball more solidly.

In 1921 the surge in hitting continued. Although no player came close to matching Babe Ruth's home run production, the gap began to narrow a bit. Players such as Rogers Hornsby, Cy Williams, Ken Williams, Bob Meusel, and Tillie Walker were finding home run ranges.

The lively-ball issue kept emerging with almost each succeeding year. In 1922, batting averages reached a new high. Home runs were increasing. Hornsby became the first player besides Ruth to reach the 40 mark in home runs. Christy Mathewson tried to put the issue to rest with this quote in the *Spalding Official Baseball Guide:*

> All this talk of a lively ball appears to be alibi stuff. The players are using long-handled bats trying for home runs because it is so popular. The bat is changed with the weight at the flying end, and the handle made thinner so that the batter can get a full grip. The old bat had a thick handle, little tapering, and the hitting was with the forearms to drive the ball through the infield. That type of swing does not produce many long fly balls.

On June 16, 1925, *The New York Times* again reported on the subject of the suspected lively ball. The National League had commissioned Harold A. Faber, a Columbia University chemistry professor with long experience in the laboratory testing of baseballs, to conduct the necessary tests to resolve the lively-ball issue. The results of this investigation were presented at a meeting of the National League owners. The *Times* stated:

> Professor Faber experimented with balls used in 1914, 1923, and 1925. After many tests he concluded that to all intents and purposes there is only a slight difference in the baseballs used in the last eleven years. . . . He offered the opinion that the improved hitting was the result of conditions that had nothing to do with a livelier ball. He listed the restrictive rules on pitching; the larger number of new balls in play; the smoother surface of the ball; and closer undercutting of the stitching of the seams, which, he concluded, conspired in favor of freer and longer hitting.

Julian Curtis, president of the A. G. Spalding Company, the manufacturer of the National League ball, also attended the meeting. As quoted in the *Times*, he said to the owners:

> "Gentlemen, I give you my word of honor there has been absolutely no change in the manufacture of the ball in recent years. Since 1919 we might have used a little better material in the way of wool yarn, otherwise the ball is exactly the same. The same weight . . . size and *resiliency*." [Emphasis added.]

The article concluded with this comment:

> It is Mr. Curtis' belief that the players are now taking toe holds and not choking up on the bats as they did in the earlier days. Evidently the fame and fortune acquired by Babe Ruth had a lot to do with the epidemic of hitting. Both Mr. Curtis and Professor Faber's statements were accepted by the National League owners, who put themselves on record that the modern baseball was not more lively than the ball of old. In short, there was no "lively ball" as the manufacturers had steadily maintained.

Barney Dreyfuss, president of the Pittsburgh club, contended that the home run craze was a result of the reduction in the sizes of the playing fields in five of the National League parks. The outfield seating, he claimed, "shortened the distances"—an obvious conclusion. This inspired a suggestion that perhaps certain drives into the outfield stands should be limited to two bases. No action was taken on that improbable notion.

Sometime later, Babe Ruth commented, as quoted in the 1925 *Reach Official Guide*: "The ball is all right. Nothing the matter with it. It's the same ball as 10 years ago. Only reason for the increased hitting, especially home runs, is that 7 of every 10 batters used to choke up on their bats—now 9 out of 10 are swinging from the hip."

Yet despite the tilt to the hitting game as influenced by Babe Ruth—and despite the climb in profits—the owners could not readily chuck their addiction to practical economics. Somewhere in the fraternity of the early-day club owners, it was decreed that the ideal ball game was one that could be played with a single baseball. Thus, a baseball fouled into the stands often touched off a melee, with club employees, police, and even the owner in relentless pursuit to retrieve the priceless object. During the course of a game, these baseballs took on a mixed set of scars. The core of the ball was softened, the cover loosened, and its color became "black as ink," as Roger Peckinpaugh, a prominent major leaguer in those days, put it.

Babe Herman, a legend in Brooklyn Dodger history, talked about that problem:

We never seemed to see a new ball. In those days the umpires were given only a dozen baseballs for a game. Can you imagine that happening today? I remember one game in Brooklyn where the first hitter fouled a ball out of the park. After that we played the entire game with only *one* baseball. I was at first base that game, and the last out was made to me. The ball was as black as the ace of spades. In those days the umpires insisted that the players return the balls to them. I managed to keep it and I still have it. Amateurs today play with cleaner balls than the one I have.

Today, it seems incredible that only *one* baseball would suffice in a major league game. No matter what the quality of materials was or how the baseball was constructed in those days, the ball was doomed by the limited number allocated to a game. Whatever resiliency those baseballs may have possessed when first put into play, they were certain to become battered, contorted, and lifeless objects by the time the game was over. If not totally dead, they sure as hell were in an acute state of moribundity.

Bibb Falk, a prominent outfielder with the Chicago White Sox and Cleveland during the twenties and thirties, said:

> I never noticed any variation in the liveliness in the ball during the years I played [1920–31]. They didn't change game balls much in those days. We were often hitting against balls that were marked up and discolored. Pitchers would squirt tobacco juice in the pocket of their gloves, which discolored the balls and made them harder to follow.

Hank Greenberg put the lively ball issue into perspective with this comment:

> I do know that the ball today [1985] is far more lively than any used in my time. I base this on the fact that so many home runs today are hit into the opposite field stands. In my day, a home run to the "off" field, for most players, was a rarity. I hit about 330 home runs in my career, and I doubt if I hit as much as a handful to the opposite field. During my years with Detroit, it was quite an achievement to hit a ball on the roof of the outfield stands in any ball park. I did it once in Comiskey Park. I recently saw an exhibition of long-ball hitting there. There were seven balls hit on the roof in that one exhibition. There is no way that can be done without a juiced-up baseball. I don't believe players today have more natural power than did Ruth, Gehrig, Foxx, Simmons, DiMaggio, Ted Williams, or myself. There were many others in the thirties who hit with power. I wish I could have had the same baseball to hit as they have now.

From 1910, when the cork-center baseball was introduced, up to 1942, when the major leagues decided to replace the shoddy, synthetic, war-time materials used in the construction of baseballs, there has never been a decree by the owners to enliven the ball. The continual claims that the players of the 1920s and 1930s were the beneficiaries of a lively ball—when in fact the ball was soft, contorted, and comparatively dead—are indicative that "Orwellian newspeak" functions in baseball, too.

Today, the liveliness of the ball is a particular center of interest. Hardly a day passes without reference by the media and the players about juiced-up baseballs. In 1987, baseballs were flying over the outfield walls at an unprecedented rate, matched only by a proliferation of explanations and rationalizations, all of which seemed to miss the mark.

There are no mysterious reasons behind the increased resilience in the current-day ball. What is overlooked is the simple fact that baseballs are manufactured items, and that manufacturing equipment of every sort is constantly improving. Baseballs today are made by state-of-the-art equipment and technology. The textile machinery in use today produces better yarns out of the same fibers that existed years ago. The yarns that go into the baseballs today are more durable, absorb more twisting, ply better, and have greater tensile strength, thus providing more liveliness to baseballs than ever before.

The manufacturers of the major league balls are not concerned with the liveliness of the baseballs, only with uniformity—no soft or dead spots. The only conditions imposed upon the makers of baseballs from the turn of the century have been the "five-and-nine" specifications. A baseball has to weigh between 5 and 5 1/4 ounces and measure between 9 and 9 1/4 inches in circumference. Dead or alive, the ball must adhere to those criteria.

As the technology in manufacturing baseballs continues to improve, the manufacturers' problems increase. The problems lie with the five-and-nine limitations. I discussed this in interviews with Doug Kralik, chief designer of the Rawlings Company, which manufactures the major league baseballs, and with Larry McClain, a vice-president of the company. Questions were posed and their answers noted, which may provide an insight to the emergence of the 1987 ball, the liveliest of its species to date.

Q: In 1910 the cork-center ball was introduced. In 1931 this was changed to a cushioned-cork center. Please explain.

A: A cork center consists of a mixture of ground-up cork and rubber, which is the core of the ball. A cushioned center consists of composition cork that is molded to layers of rubber and then applied to the core.

Q: Why is this cushion important?

A: The cushion provides uniformity to the baseball, which is our basic aim. We avoid contortions.

Q: Does this cushion also increase the resiliency of the ball?

A: Probably, although that is not our primary concern.

Q: How was the cushion constructed when first introduced in 1931?

A: We don't know what the construction process was in 1931. Apparently, it didn't do the job, since those balls developed soft spots and contortions.

Q: Assuming that the baseballs used in the 1920s and 1930s lacked the uniformity that exists today, can you conceive how that might have resulted in a livelier baseball?

A: No. The opposite would be true. Those balls would have "dead" spots and, of course, be less lively.

Q: There have been times in the past when the stitching in the National League ball was raised. This change provided pitchers with a better grip and gave them a big edge against the hitters. Could this happen today?

A: No. Every baseball we construct goes through a rolling machine process that eliminates any raised seams.

Q: How good is the quality of the yarns that go into the baseball?

A: We use the best quality.

Q: That means longer-staple wool and cotton fibers, which permit greater twisting, which produces harder yarns, resulting in greater tensile strength. Hence, a livelier ball. Is that right?

A: Up to a point. If the cavity of the ball is filled to the maximum with hard yarns, the weight of the ball would exceed the five-ounce limit. And, of course, we can't reduce the nine-inch circumference.

Q: However, if you removed some of the hard yarns and substituted with lighter-weight materials, such as more cork and rubber, wouldn't that give you a five-ounce ball with maximum resiliency?

A: Let's say that is a good analysis.

The so-called lively ball of the 1920s and 1930s, is pure fiction. What has led the baseball pundits down this blind path is their inability to account for the higher batting averages in those years, compared to batting averages today. They are particularly baffled by the .303 average of the National League in 1930. How was that possible if not with a lively ball?

4 Baseball's Most Durable, Most Overlooked Record

"For anybody to do what they did in 1930...that ball had to be juiced."
Ralph Kiner, quoted in Baseball for the Love of It,
by Anthony J. Connor

No sport provides the fascination with records that baseball does—Babe Ruth's 60 home runs, Ty Cobb's 4,191 hits and his .367 lifetime average, Joe DiMaggio's 56-consecutive-game hitting streak, just for openers. Ruth's record has been broken, and Cobb's 4,191 hits have been overtaken by Pete Rose, and will probably be superseded again in years to come. Even DiMaggio's record has been threatened and may eventually be erased.

There is, however, one other record that has never been recognized or understood and whose immortality is assured above all others—the .303 batting average achieved by the National League in 1930. It was the greatest display of batting firepower in the history of baseball and a valid accomplishment for the league. Yet this incredible feat has been slighted, discounted, and maligned by skeptical baseball writers and statisticians. They cannot accept the reality of the event. Thus, they resurrect that tenacious myth, the lively ball. Only a lively ball could have produced that astonishing result.

The Hidden Game of Baseball, by Thorn and Palmer, states: "1930 was the year in which the National League officials, attempting to match the popularity of the slugging American League, *juiced the baseball to an extent that the entire league batted .312.*" (Emphasis added) The National League average was of course .303, not .312. The authors evidently felt that by deleting the pitchers and their batting averages, a more improbable statistic would be created.

The .303 National League average in 1930 was a record breaker. But so was the .294 average the year before. The jump of 9 points between 1929 and 1930, however, was not unusual. Nor was it the largest gain from one year to another. The league had experienced a 19-point increase in 1921; a 9-point increase in 1925; and a rise of 13 points in 1929.

The American League hit .288 in 1930, which was not much different from most of their previous years. For them, 1930 was just another year.

If the .303 batting average in the National League in 1930 alarmed the owners, it was not evident at their annual league meetings on December 9 and 10, 1930. The minutes state: "There was much discussion at the meeting concerning the baseballs but it did not result in any definite action. Some of the members thought the ball was faster than it had been."

The 1930 baseball may have appeared faster, as some of the National League members believed. But this surmise flies in the face of the decision at the previous meeting in December 1929. Those minutes stated: "It was decided that if the makers of the baseball could remove the gloss from it, the pitchers would profit by a presumable advantage. *No changes were considered in the composition of the baseball nor were any asked for.*" (Emphasis added)

The gloss was removed by having the umpires rub the baseballs with a special mud before each game—a seemingly small yet distinct advantage to the pitchers. The apparent intent was to curtail hitting in 1930, not to expand it.

The remarkable .303 average for the National League in 1930 was the result of a number of factors that converged in that particular year, none of them having anything to do with a "juiced-up" baseball. That record may astonish people today, but at the time it made little impact on the fans and the media. During the 1920s, they saw individual clubs in both leagues hit over .300 on 24 occasions. They saw the leagues' averages reach .290 or better 6 times. They were inured to good hitting and were not overwhelmed when one of the leagues finally broke the .300 mark. They were expecting it.

.300 AVERAGES FOR INDIVIDUAL CLUBS, 1920–29

1920	A.L.	St. Louis	.308
		Cleveland	.303
1921	A.L.	Detroit	.316
		Cleveland	.308
		St. Louis	.304
		New York	.300
1922	A.L.	St. Louis	.313
		Detroit	.305
	N.L.	Pittsburgh	.308
		New York	.304
		St. Louis	.301
1923	A.L.	Cleveland	.301
		Detroit	.300
1924	N.L.	New York	.300
1925	A.L.	Philadelphia	.307
		Washington	.303
		Detroit	.302
	N.L.	Pittsburgh	.307
1927	A.L.	New York	.307
		Philadelphia	.303
	N.L.	Pittsburgh	.305
1928	N.L.	Pittsburgh	.309
1929	N.L.	Pittsburgh	.303
		Chicago	.303

The phenomenal hitting in 1930 had its roots in 1920. The batting exploits of Babe Ruth effected changes in batting styles which produced long-ball hitting, greater fan interest, and the

BATTING AVERAGES 1920–29

	National	American
1920	.270	.283
1921	.289	.292
1922	.292	.284
1923	.286	.282
1924	.283	.290
1925	.292	.292
1926	.280	.281
1927	.282	.285
1928	.281	.281
1929	.294	.284

construction of outfield bleachers and stands to accommodate the increase in attendance. With the new seating, balls that previously would have been caught were now settling into the stands for home runs or were bouncing off the walls for extra-base hits.

Batting averages began to climb. The ban on illegal pitching and the reduction in the outfield dimensions provided an obvious boost to batting averages. But the greatest importance was the accumulation of extraordinarily talented players, culminating in 1930 with the largest number of Hall of Fame players in the major leagues in any one year.

From 1920 through 1939, there were 68 ultimate Hall of Fame players performing in the major leagues. That was more than four times as many Hall of Fame players than in any other 20-year span in baseball's history. Thirty-seven of these 68 players were playing in that one historic year, 1930 (30 position players and 7 pitchers). The list does not include 7 additional Hall of Fame players who were still active and effective but past their prime years: Rogers Hornsby, Harry Heilmann, George Kelly, Rabbit Maranville, George Sisler, Red Faber, Waite Hoyt, and Eppa Rixey.

HALL OF FAME PLAYERS IN 1930
Position Players

Earl Averill	Lou Gehrig	Mel Ott
Jim Bottomley	Charlie Gehringer	Sam Rice
Mickey Cochrane	Goose Goslin	Babe Ruth
Earle Combs	Chick Hafney	Joe Sewell
Joe Cronin	Gabby Hartnett	Al Simmons
Kiki Cuyler	Travis Jackson	Bill Terry
Bill Dickey	Chuck Klein	Pie Traynor
Rick Ferrell	Freddie Lindstrom	Lloyd Waner
Jimmie Foxx	Al Lopez	Paul Waner
Frankie Frisch	Heinie Manush	Hack Wilson

In addition, the major leagues in 1930, were studded with supporting players who were not far removed from Hall of Fame quality. What would club owners give today to own the contracts of the following players of 1930?

Wally Berger	Charlie Grimm	Bob O'Farrell
Ossie Bluege	Rollie Hemsley	Jimmie Reese
Ben Chapman	Babe Herman	Carl Reynolds
Doc Cramer	Joe Judge	Riggs Stephenson
Spud Davis	Willie Kamm	John Stone
Taylor Douthit	Tony Lazzeri	Gus Suhr
Leo Durocher	Gus Mancuso	Earl Webb
Jimmy Dykes	Bing Miller	Pinky Whitney
Woody English	Buddy Myer	Jimmie Wilson
George Grantham	Lefty O'Doul	Glenn Wright

All conclusions in this book are based upon hitting alone. No system has ever been devised, much less proven, that can accurately measure the quality of defense from one year to another, let alone over a 20-year period. It can, however, reasonably be assumed that the 20-year span from 1920 through 1939 that produced exceptional hitting talent would also include an equal measure of proficiency in fielding and pitching.

In 1930, the hitters faced an array of exceptional pitchers, Hall of Famers such as Jesse Haines, Burleigh Grimes, Carl Hubbell, Dazzy Vance, Bob Grove, Red Ruffing, and Ted Lyons. Non–Hall of Fame pitchers such as George Earnshaw, Freddie Fitzsimmons, Wes Ferrell, Bill Walker, Bill Hallahan, Firpo Marberry, Mel Harder, and Earl Whitehill were also no cinch for any of the hitters. Joe DiMaggio once commented that Mel Harder was the toughest pitcher he ever faced. Ever hear of him? Ask those who played with him or against him about Mel Harder's pitching ability. Or about the pitching ability of Willis Hudlin, or George Earnshaw, or Ray Kremer.

Most fans understand the value to a ball club of one outstanding player—a superstar. But that one player is often severely handicapped. Pitchers pitch around him. He seldom gets a good ball to hit, especially with men on base. These hitters are often forced to swing at bad balls in their zeal to be productive. They don't have the benefit of being backed up with another menacing hitter, ideally a hitter who swings from the opposite side of the plate. For example, the lack of a consistent, companion hitting threat put a real burden on such players as Wally Berger and Ralph Kiner. This was also the fate of Dave Winfield when with the San Diego Padres. The results achieved by these players, under those circumstances, are a flattering measure of their ability.

Two-player combinations, though, are an entirely different story. The impact of at least two good hitters, back to back, is the basis for a winning club. They set the pace, provide the leadership, and generate confidence among the remaining players. Of course, defense and decent pitching are prerequisites, but the value of a combination of two solid hitters cannot be overestimated.

Many fans will recall the accomplishments of later partnerships that brought championships to their teams: Mathews/Aaron (Milwaukee); Mays/McCovey (San Francisco); Mantle/Maris (Yankees); Perez/Bench (Cincinnati); Killebrew/Oliva (Minnesota); Garvey/Cey (Los Angeles); Schmidt/Luzinski (Philadelphia); Murray/Ripken (Baltimore). The twenties and thirties were stocked with such combination. That was another distinguishing feature of those early years.

The table below illustrates the impact of the back-to-back combination. In the 13 years that the Waner brothers played with Pittsburgh, for example, they alone raised their team average by 11 points. The Babe Ruth–Lou Gehrig combination, in a period of 10 years (1925–34), increased the average of their team by 12

TWO-PLAYER COMBINATIONS, 1920–39

Two-Player Combinations	Years Played on Same Team	Combined Average	Overall Team Average	Team Average without the Two Players
1920–26				
Cobb-Heilmann	7	.363	.297	.281
1925–34				
Ruth-Gehrig	10	.345	.291	.279
1925–32				
Simmons-Foxx	8	.353	.293	.281
1920–27				
Sisler-K. Williams	8	.342	.294	.283
1926–36				
Terry-Ott	11	.333	.287	.276
1933–39				
Greenberg-Gehringer	7	.332	.286	.275
1927–39				
P. Waner-L. Waner	13	.331	.289	.278
1921–30				
Goslin-Rice	10	.327	.287	.276
Total	74			

points. In the process, they led the Yankees to five pennants, with four second-place finishes and one third-place finish.

All of the above players (except Ken Williams) are Hall of Famers, and with good reason. The aggregate period of time for all these combinations totaled 74 years. During those years their teams finished:

In 1st place	13 times
In 2nd place	16 times
In 3rd place	12 times
In 4th place	9 times
Total	50 times

In 1930, many great hitting combinations flourished in the National League. Bottomley, Frisch, Hafey, and Watkins with St. Louis; Cuyler, Wilson, Stephenson, and Hartnett with the Cubs; Terry, Ott, Lindstrom, and Jackson with the Giants; Herman, Bissonette, and Wright with Brooklyn; the Waners, Traynor, and Grantham with Pittsburgh; and Klein, O'Doul, and Whitney with the Phillies. Only Boston and Cincinnati lacked powerful hitting combinations in 1930— Boston relying upon Wally Berger and an aging Sisler to carry them, while Harry Heilmann and Cuccinello had to bear the load for Cincinnati. These 26 National League players averaged .368 among them, an achievement that induced the record-breaking .303 average that year.

As it turned out, 1930 was the apex of the Ruthian era. What made that year noteworthy was the breaking of the .300 barrier. What highlighted that record was the collapse in hitting the next year, 1931. Those were two of the most unusual years in baseball: a record breaker one year and the largest drop-off in hitting the next year.

The collapse in hitting in 1931 was due directly to changes

in the construction of the baseball. The first change was the introduction of the cushioned cork-center ball. The intent of the cushion was to remove any contortions in the ball, to make it rebound to its original shape. The second change was raising the seams on the ball.

Both leagues adopted the cushioned baseball, but the raised seams were exclusive with the National League. The cushion did not eliminate the contortions in the baseball. That experiment failed, producing instead a softer baseball. The ball became more dead and thus less resilient. Batting averages plummeted. The disparity in the ball's resilience between 1930 and 1931, was clearly evident. Power hitters are generally high-fly hitters. Most often, their long drives have enough loft and intensity to carry into the stands or rattle off the outfield fences. In 1931 the deadened ball hung in the air.

Babe Herman suffered by it. He recalled: "We were playing in Pittsburgh one day, and I hit a long drive to right field. I thought, for sure, the ball was gone. Instead, Cuyler comes in and makes the catch. I couldn't believe it. It was the third out. On his way in, Cuyler shows me the ball. It had a flat spot."

In 1930 Wally Berger hit 38 home runs for the Boston Braves, establishing himself as one of the premier home run hitters in the game. The next year, 1931, his home run production fell to 19. He explained: "The big difference was in the baseball. The ball was dead in 1931. I remember hitting a ball one day that I just knew was a home run. I was amazed to see the left fielder make an easy catch of it. That happened several times to me."

Deadening the baseball in 1931 by the introduction of an ineffective cushion was bad enough. Raising the seams on the National League ball compounded the problem for the hitters. To the pitchers, raising the seams was an edge comparable to increasing the strike zone or shortening the distance to the plate.

What was once an ordinary curveball now became a sharp breaking pitch that often came at a hitter as if falling off a table. Home runs are hit mostly off fastballs, if for no other reason than this pitch is thrown more often. A decent curveball, or any "breaking" ball, invariably puts a hitter off stride enough to reduce power in the swing. (Of course, home runs are also hit off curves and other "breaking" pitches, especially when such pitches hang or are misdirected.) The raised seams on the 1931 ball in the National League became a nightmare for the hitters. That was the year the National League acquired its reputation as a curveball league.

Al Lopez had this to say about the raised seams:

> In 1931 they raised the seams on the National League ball. We still had good hitting, but the power hitters especially were not getting as many fastballs to hit. The curveballs were breaking sharper and were thrown more often. It hurt power hitters such as Hack Wilson, Wally Berger, and Babe Herman. I had some problems, too. Balls that I hit against the stands or into them in 1930 were now lazy outs.

The National League suffered the most. By adding the raised seams to an ineffectively cushioned ball, they suffered a 26-point drop in the league's batting average. Their home run production dropped almost in half. The American League, which did not adopt the raised-seam baseball, had only a 10-point loss in its averages and a 15 percent drop in home runs. This was the first time in 10 years that the National League hit fewer home runs than the American League. In fact, through the last 9 years of the decade (1931–39), the National League never again led in either batting average or home runs.

Although the combined major leagues never again reached the overall average of .285 in the 1920s, their hitting records in the next decade were no cause for embarrassment. From 1931 through 1939, four American League clubs reached the .300 mark, with the combined leagues achieving a respectable .279 average, an accomplishment never duplicated thereafter.

This .279 major league average is 19 points higher than the .260 average achieved from 1980 through 1987. The major reason for this disparity resides in the most negative and least understood statistic in baseball—the strikeout.

5 The Strikeout—Baseball's Most Positive Negative

"I believe there are 10 men in the majors today who can hit .400 if they would try to hit the ball past the fielders and not out of the park."
—Branch Rickey, 1960

The impact of strikeouts on the outcome of a baseball game cannot be overstated. The strikeout is baseball's most damaging, most deleterious contributor to the nonproduction of runs. It is exactly what it implies—a cipher, a zero without a single redeeming feature. Even a double play, damaging as it is, may produce a run—the strikeout, never. With the exception of an inept defense, nothing is more counterproductive to the objective of winning a game.

Earl Weaver, a long-time manager of the Baltimore Orioles, extolled the value of the three-run home run. What he indirectly stressed was the importance of the big innings, which usually determine the outcome of a game. Most fans are aware that in the majority of cases—Ralph Kiner estimates it at 70 percent—the winning team will score more runs in one inning than the loser will in the entire game. What does this have to do with strikeouts? Everything.

For the most part, a baseball game consists of routine innings, three up and three down, interspersed with an occasional walk, hit, or run. But in every game, critical situations develop that rise in importance far above those routine innings. They are the "clutch" innings that invariably determine the outcome of a game. They invariably make their presence known in the course of a batting rally. To the team that is at bat, it is vital to sustain the rally in order to produce the big inning. In the midst of a potentially big inning, nothing will blunt the rally and negate the flow of runs more effectively than a strikeout.

A few years ago, Richie Allen, a player who racked up an impressive number of home runs and an even more impressive number of strikeouts, was quoted in a San Diego paper as counseling a Padre hitter: "It doesn't matter if you strike out 200 times a year. You're going to make that many outs one way or another."

Modern-day players do not seem overly concerned with their excessive strikeouts. Chili Davis, an outfielder with the 1988 California Angels, gave his views on strikeouts in an article in the *Los Angeles Times* on May 22, 1988:

> Right now, I'm being a little more aggressive with the bat. I figure if I strike out, big deal. It seems like I've got a hundred strikeouts already. If I get a hundred more, what the hell. . . .

Even some managers are not troubled by strikeouts. In a quote in *The Sporting News* a few years ago, Steve Boros, who was managing Oakland at the time, commented: "I never figured out why striking out is worse than popping up. It's still an out." That may be one reason why Boros isn't managing a ball club anymore.

There is a huge psychological advantage for a pitcher who strikes out a hitter, especially in a critical part of the game. He has mastered the hitter in a way that cannot be duplicated by inducing an out by a batted ball.

Ferris Fain, a good hitter in his day, is not exactly an old-timer of the twenties and thirties, but his major league career goes back 40 years, to 1947. In an interview, he observed: "The problem with strikeouts is that they not only break up and destroy the momentum of a rally but they give a lift to the pitcher. Once you get a pitcher on the ropes you don't want to let up."

Most major league managers and executives dread strikeouts by their players more than any other act in baseball. Al Lopez said: "When I was managing, nothing distressed me more than having a player of mine strike out in the middle of a batting rally. It would kill the rally, and suddenly we got a tougher pitcher facing us."

In 1984 Steve Balboni of the Kansas City Royals tied a major league record by striking out an incredible nine straight times, swinging at and missing 20 pitches in the process. It's hard to imagine a major league player missing that many pitches in nine consecutive times at bat. Balboni must have been swinging with a sword. Commenting on his first baseman's proclivity for striking out, Dick Howser, a highly successful manager of the Kansas City team, made this unusual statement: "I know he's going to set an American League record for strikeouts but it doesn't bother me and it doesn't bother him. He's a legitimate 30-[homers]-a-year guy, and once you're in that range, you're a title contender."

Let's see. Balboni strikes out at the rate of once in every 3 times at bat. He hits a home run once in every 16 times at bat—or once in every four games. It would be interesting to record the lost opportunities for runs, and the batting rallies that were aborted by Balboni's strikeouts, and to measure those failures against the home runs he hits. Dick Howser undoubtedly would have gladly traded half of Balboni's home runs for a 50 percent reduction in his strikeouts.

Earl Weaver's dream of the three-run homer is every manager's ideal. But most players are not home run types, and the three-run homer is a small fraction when calculated among the 37,000 base hits produced in an average season.

The simple object in baseball is to win games. This can only be accomplished by scoring more runs than the opposition, by whatever means are available. The home run is *not* the most important indicator of scoring runs. Base hits, other than home runs, are far more productive. In modern-day baseball, major league clubs average 10 times as many smaller hits than home runs. In the vast majority of cases, critical game situations require and are won by only a timely single, a fly ball, or even a ground ball. Home runs are dramatic and they do win ball games; but the less dramatic little hits are more influential in determining the outcome of a game.

Swinging for the fences does not necessarily add more home runs. What swinging for the fences is more likely to produce is ineffective hitting and a greater number of strikeouts, resulting in a decrease in base hits, runs scored, and games won.

The formula is clear: Fewer strikeouts produce more base hits, which produce more runs, which produce more winning games, which produce higher positions in the standings. Isn't that the objective of major league baseball?

There is direct correlation between the zeal for home runs and the mounting proliferation of strikeouts. In the combined American and National leagues, the year 1987 produced a record number 4,458 home runs, an average of 171 homers per team. This was more than twice the team average of the twenties and thirties. Yet in RBIs, where it mattered most, the majors in 1987 were less productive than the teams in the Ruthian years. The team average in 1987 was 675 RBIs; in the 1920s and 1930s it was 685 RBIs per team. Although the difference of 10 RBIs per team is minuscule, the important point is that home runs are not necessarily the biggest producer of runs.

In 1987, the combined leagues struck out 25,098 times, the largest number of strikeouts in any year in history. That total adjusted to conform to 16 teams playing a 154-game schedule, equates to 14,657 strikeouts, approximately twice the 7.517 strike-outs recorded in an average year in the twenties and thirties. One need not be a knowledgeable fan, much less a statistician, to grasp the importance of that statistic. Those extra 7,140 strikeouts in 1987 were at a cost of approximately 1,850 base hits, which could have increased the leagues' batting average by a significant 8 to 10 points. More importantly, these additional hits would have produced more runs and more wins in the win–loss columns for many of the clubs.

The trend in strikeouts is growing. In 1987, there were 41 players who struck out more than 100 times, setting a record in that category. By comparison, in the entire 20 years from 1920 through 1939, 100 or more strikeouts occurred only 10 times: This included 5 by Dolf Camilli and 2 by Vince DiMaggio.

100 OR MORE STRIKEOUTS—COMBINED LEAGUES
(Adjusted to 16 teams, 154-game schedule)
1920–39 (20 years):   10 Times
1987 (1 year):   25 Times

In the one year, 1987, there have been two and a half times as many players with 100 strikeouts than in the entire 20-year span from 1920 through 1939. If we compare 1987 with the annual average for those 20 years, the result is an astonishing 50:1 ratio.

Of course, not all strikeouts can be avoided. Some pitchers are at times unhittable, even by the best hitters. When Carl Hubbell struck out five great hitters in a row in an All-Star game, it was Hubbell's pitching ability and his specialty, the screwball, that made those strikeouts possible. When gifted pitchers have their good stuff going for them, nobody is going to hit them and strikeouts will pile up.

Sandy Koufax is a good example. He recorded strikeouts not so much through the ineffectiveness of the hitters as with his superlative pitching equipment—a hard, rising fastball, an exploding curve, and above all, great deception. His pitches were thrown with identical overhand deliveries. There have been and always will be pitchers with the special talent of producing strikeouts. But they are in the minority.

"There are more strikeouts today because modern-day pitchers throw harder." Who says so? Only those who have never seen baseball in earlier years. Bibb Falk's comment may speak for all the old-timers. He asked, "Hasn't anybody heard of Walter Johnson and Bob Grove? How do you suppose they racked up all those strikeouts, 12 to 15 a game in the daytime? How did Bob Feller do it?"

How good a pitcher was Feller? In 1936 the trainer for the Washington Senators was Mike Martin, an old-timer who had been with the club when Walter Johnson was in his prime. He idolized Johnson and boasted about Johnson's fastball, which he claimed was the best of all time. The players would tease Mike about his fixation with Johnson's fastball. He would take the bait and respond with a typical comment about other fastball pitchers: "They couldn't carry Johnson's glove."

Late in that 1936 season, during the last few innings of a game with Cleveland, with darkness setting in, those of us on the bench could see a tall, awkward-looking pitcher warming up in the bullpen. He twirled his arm over his head, kicked his leg up to his chin, uncoiled, and released his pitch. We could hear the loud pop of a ball cracking into the catcher's glove. But no ball was visible. It was eerie. That's when Mike Martin made this surprising statement: "That's the only fastball I've seen that compares with Walter." The pitcher was Bob Feller, who was about to enter the game and pitch his first inning in a regular major league game.

There's never been a hitter who likes to hit against a wild, ungainly, hard-throwing rookie. Feller's motion seemed to be a conglomeration of unconnected parts, moving toward the hitter from all directions. The first hitter to face him was my roommate, Buddy Lewis. Lewis was a left-handed hitter, a dead-right-field pull hitter who, it was said, couldn't throw a ball into left field. Against Feller, Buddy Lewis established a first for himself—he

53

popped up to the third baseman. He couldn't get his bat around on Feller's fastball. The next hitter was Cecil Travis, a good hitter who rarely struck out. Feller got him on strikes. The third hitter was Ben Chapman, who was observing all this with typical skepticism. He was determined to tear into Feller's fastball. He too went down on strikes. That was the start of Bob Feller's career; Feller went on to become one of baseball's greatest strikeout pitchers. In his debut he was the scariest pitcher any hitter could face. He possessed a fastball comparable to Walter Johnson's and a curveball comparable to none.

When reading the drivel of the new breed of baseball pundits who deprecate the pitching talent of the twenties and thirties, which they never saw, one has only to think of Bob Feller and the strikeouts he posted in his career. How would players today react if they had to face the assortment of stuff Feller threw at hitters in 1936 and in subsequent years?

One of baseball's misconceptions is the linkage of home runs and excessive strikeouts—as if you can't have one without the other. They are not concomitant. Home runs are hit off pitches in the strike zone, in a hitter's wheelhouse. Strikeouts are what you get by swinging at pitches out of the strike zone. At best, swinging at bad balls produces ineffective contact with the ball. Batting averages and home runs are directly and adversely affected by the incidence of strikeouts.

The table below illustrates the relationship between batting average, home runs, and strikeouts, by presenting the records of those Hall of Fame players with 300 or more home runs. Also included are Carl Yastrzemski, Mike Schmidt, Johnny Bench, and Reggie Jackson, who are reasonably certain to be inducted into the Hall of Fame when eligible.

In evaluating the relationship between strikeouts and batting averages for these 30 players, a more logical approach was taken to eliminate distortions that arise from the varying lengths of players' careers. Obviously, a player with a 20-year career will have compiled more hits, more home runs, and more strikeouts than a 10-year player of equal ability. To accurately determine the comparable achievements of these players, a standard of 500 at-bats has been established to represent a year's play. (No consideration is given to walks or the number of times a player was hit by a pitch.)

By dividing this standard of 500 at-bats into a player's actual total of at-bat appearances, the number of "years" played can be calculated for the purposes of comparison. Thus, for example, Babe Ruth's 22 years in the major leagues are condensed to 16¾ years. Hank Greenberg's 13 years are reduced to 10⅓; Ted Williams' from 19 to 15½.

Sometimes these calculations go into reverse, as in the cases of Hank Aaron and Carl Yastrzemski. Their careers included many 162-game seasons, resulting in a comparatively higher number of at-bats in a season. The 500-at-bat formula increases such players' tenures. Both Aaron's and Yastrzemski's years in the majors expand from 23 to 24.

The table reveals a particularly interesting picture of how Mickey Mantle's career was affected by his excessive strikeouts. Mantle was a true superstar, a winner, and a courageous player who suffered a variety of injuries without complaint during his years with the New York Yankees (1951 through 1968). His induction into baseball's Hall of Fame in his first year of eligibility was the ultimate tribute for this exceptional player.

Mantle was endowed with more natural physical attributes than perhaps any player in baseball's history. With the exception of Babe Ruth, no player had more batting power than Mantle. He had the enormous advantage of being a switch-hitter with extra-

BATTING AVERAGE AND HOME RUNS VS. STRIKEOUTS*

Hall of Fame Players	Years Played	Lifetime Batting Average	Strikeouts Per Year	Home Runs Per Year
Rogers Hornsby	16⅓	.358	42	18
Ted Williams	15½	.344	46	34
Babe Ruth	16¾	.342	79	43
Lou Gehrig	16	.340	49	31
Stan Musial	22	.331	32	22
Joe DiMaggio	13½	.325	27	27
Jimmie Foxx	16¼	.325	81	33
Chuck Klein	13	.320	40	23
Al Simmons	17½	.320	42	18
Hank Greenberg	10⅓	.313	81	32
Johnny Mize	14	.312	40	28
Hank Aaron	24½	.305	56	31
Mel Ott	19	.304	48	27
Willie Mays	21¾	.302	70	30
Mickey Mantle	16¼	.298	105	33
Al Kaline	20	.297	50	20
Billy Williams	18¾	.295	56	23
Duke Snider	14⅓	.295	87	28
Frank Robinson	20	.294	76	29
Carl Yastrzemski	24	.285	59	19
Yogi Berra	15	.285	28	24
Willie Stargell	15¾	.282	122	30
Ralph Kiner	10½	.279	72	35
Ernie Banks	18½	.274	66	28
Eddie Mathews	17	.271	87	30
Mike Schmidt**	15½	.270	117	35
Willie McCovey	16½	.270	95	32
Johnny Bench	15⅓	.267	84	25
Reggie Jackson	19¾	.262	129	30
Harmon Killebrew	16¼	.256	105	35

*Through 1987; 300-home-run minimum; 500 at-bats equals one year.
**Still active in 1988.

ordinary speed from either side of the plate. He had the innate talent and the potential to have become the greatest hitter ever to wear a major league uniform.

But the lack of one major ingredient plagued Mantle throughout his career: a good familiarity with the strike zone. Predictably, this resulted in an excessive number of strikeouts. His yearly average of 105 strikeouts would have been too many for a player of ordinary talent. For a supertalented player such as Mantle, 105 strikeouts a year was almost beyond belief.

A 50 percent reduction in Mantle's strikeouts would have been in line with the strikeout average of the 14 players above him on the list. It would have boosted his average to approximately .330, a not unreasonable expectation for a player with his unique physical gifts. With greater discipline at the plate, given his switch-hitting and remarkable speed, even a .350 to .375 lifetime average could have been within Mantle's reach. Being more selective at the plate would have produced more good pitches for Mantle, more pitches in his wheelhouse, and the likelihood of more home runs.

In his book *My Turn at Bat*, Ted Williams, an admirer of Mantle, said: "I used to think Al Kaline or Mantle could have hit .400. But Mantle missed the ball too much. Too many strikeouts. He was forever going for the long ball, even with two strikes."

There is no easy explanation for Mantle's inability to define the strike zone. Perhaps he was brought up to the majors prematurely. One more year in the minors might have made a difference.

Mickey Mantle himself expressed it best in a poignant reflection on his career in his book, *Mick*: ". . . god-damn, to think you're a .300 hitter and . . . find yourself looking at a lifetime .298 average—it made me want to cry."

Much is often made of Babe Ruth's "majestic" and supposedly excessive strikeouts. Yet few people realize that this never-to-be-equaled slugger struck out 90 times only twice in his long career. As the table indicates, he averaged only 79 strikeouts a year. There are singles hitters today who strike out far more often than Babe Ruth. *The Baseball Encyclopedia* lists the 35 players with the highest ratio of strikeouts to times at bat. Babe Ruth is not among them. In fact, not a single player of the 1920s and 1930s appears on that list.

Reggie Jackson is the prototype of the modern-day superstar and ticketed for the Hall of Fame. His claims to fame are his charisma, his 583 home runs spanning a 20-year career, and hitting 3 home runs in a World Series game, thus earning the title of Mr. October.

Yet Jackson's most notable, but unrecognized, legacy to base-ball is his influence in removing the stigma of strikeouts in the game. His 583 home runs are an achievement. But not so his lifetime .263 batting average or his 2,597 strikeouts.

He also has the dubious distinction of having struck out 600 more times than any other player in history, with more strikeouts than Babe Ruth, Lou Gehrig, and Joe DiMaggio combined. His strikeouts become even more dismal considering that he had the solid advantage of hitting exclusively against right-handed pitching for five years, as a designated hitter. It is a reasonable assumption that Jackson's strikeouts give him the unenviable record of having stranded more men on base than any player ever to play the game. Despite his negative accomplishments, some writers have guaranteed Jackson a niche in the Hall of Fame on the first ballot of his eligibility, an honor that has never been assured for any other player.

The strikeout has become a non-event in baseball today, not only for the home run hitters but also for "singles" hitters. In the twenties and thirties, striking out was a humiliating experience for a player. For the average player, a propensity for striking out meant a short major league stay and a ticket to the minor leagues. Even a superstar player such as Wally Berger was distressed by his number of strikeouts, which would be considered modest in current-day baseball: "In 1933 I struck out 77 times, leading the league in that department. It was my most embarrassing experience in baseball."

That comment is from a player who hit .313 that year, with 27 home runs—while driving in 106 runs on a ball club without another big hitter to carry the load. Just as with Ralph Kiner, Berger rarely had a good ball to hit with men on base. Pitchers worked around him.

Branch Rickey's comment about the possibility of hitting .400 if players "didn't try to hit the ball out of the ball park" is not quite on target. It is the tendency for striking out that has made the .400 hitter extinct and is bringing the .300 hitter closer to a vanishing species.

A glance at the table of the seven .400 hitters dating from 1911, reveals the remarkably low number of strikeouts they incurred.

.400 HITTERS

		AB	Hits	SO	Average
*Cobb	(1911)	591	248		.420
*Jackson	(1911)	571	233		.408
*Cobb	(1912)	553	227		.410
**Jackson	(1920)	570	218	14	.382
Sisler	(1920)	631	257	19	.407
Sisler	(1922)	586	246	14	.420
Cobb	(1922)	526	211	24	.401
Hornsby	(1922)	623	250	50	.401
Heilmann	(1923)	524	211	40	.403
Hornsby	(1924)	536	227	32	.424
Hornsby	(1925)	504	203	39	.403
Terry	(1930)	606	254	33	.401
Williams	(1941)	456	185	27	.406

*No record of strikeouts.
**Jackson's best year after strikeouts were recorded.

Even if these players had doubled their strikeouts, it would have been respectable by today's standards. But they would have produced fewer hits and their teams would have lost more games. How many hits would they have lost by an increase in their strikeouts? We'll let the statisticians speculate with those probabilities. It is not, however, a matter of speculation that base hits are not possible when striking out.

Two questions come to mind. Why do the modern-day players strike out so much? How can strikeouts be reduced so as to provide more productivity? These questions were posed to prominent veteran major-league players and managers.

Al Lopez contends:

> Much of the problem with today's hitters is that they're too far from the plate. Thus, they enlarge the strike zone and make it easier on the pitchers. The toughest hitters to pitch to are those who crowd the plate. The hitter who is so far from the plate that his bat can't reach the outside of the plate is the easiest to strike out.

Babe Herman expressed another view:

> It's not so much where a batter stands at the plate that counts, as it is the bat coverage of the plate. One thing all good hitters have in common is good bat coverage of the plate and short strides. Joe DiMaggio and Mel Ott had practically no stride at all. They seemed to just pick up their front foot and put it back in the same spot.

Hank Greenberg saw it this way:

> The biggest problem I see is that many players don't have a good idea of the strike zone. They swing at pitches not only off the plate, but even in the dirt. This comes back to a lack of seasoning—not enough minor league experience. In the major leagues, pitchers don't pitch down the middle of the plate as they may do in the minors. A major league pitcher won't hesitate to throw a breaking ball when behind in the count. In the minors they don't see it that often or expect it. Further, too many hitters are swinging for home runs when they're

not the type. They may get a homer now and then, but they pay a big price by running up an excessive number of strikeouts.

Johnnie Kerr said:

A hitter must get a piece of the ball, especially when the game is on the line. The worst thing you can do is strike out. You've put a hole in your batting rally. There are lots of things a hitter can do to keep from striking out. The most common maneuver is to get closer to the plate and cut down on your swing. This is not defensive hitting, as much as recognizing the situation and accommodating yourself to it. All the great hitters in baseball made adjustments in their stances and swings in these situations. Eddie Collins was the best I ever saw at adjusting at the plate. He could foul off pitches all day until he got a pitch that he liked. Not all players were as good as Collins, but every player knew the importance of protecting the plate. I don't know why players don't do that today with two strikes on them.

Did Babe Ruth ever cut down on his swing or change his stance at the plate? "Rarely," said Jimmie Reese:

I remember only one time when that happened. We were playing Washington and evidently they came up with a special strategy for stopping the Babe from hitting home runs. They would challenge him to hit to left field by moving Bluege in from third base . . . 20 or 30 feet closer to the plate. Ruth was determined to drive the ball down Bluege's throat. Lloyd Brown, a left-hander, was pitching for Washington, and he kept crowding pitches in on Ruth's hands. Ruth kept swinging at Bluege, but all that happened was pop flies to the infield. I remember Pennock shouting at the Babe to forget it and swing naturally. But Ruth was stubborn. The last time up, Brown got the ball over the outside of the plate and Ruth hit it over the left field wall. When he returned to the dugout he was unhappy about the home run. "That's not what I wanted," he complained. "I wanted to hit that little bastard at third base. He was trying to show me up." Babe Ruth never thought about strikeouts. He felt he could hit anyone.

I discussed strikeouts with a manager in the majors today who asked not to be identified:

Players are striking out a lot these days for one main reason. Many of them, even experienced players, lack knowledge of the strike zone. For the young player, it's a matter of not having enough minor league experience. They all want to be home-run hitters, so they're down at the end of the bat. The home run is important to them, and they rarely think about adjusting with two strikes.

When asked about the preponderance of strikeouts in baseball today, Bibb Falk said:

When I joined the White Sox directly from college in the middle of 1920, all I did was sit around and watch some pretty good ball players in action. That Joe Jackson was impressive. A perfect swing. How he could drive that ball and yet not strike out. When that team was broken up in 1921, I figured I could take up the slack, but I had no idea of the strike zone. By the time the year was over, I had struck out 69 times, which was too much. The next year was not much better, although I hit a few more homers. Finally, I decided to stop swinging for the fences. That's when things began to pick up for me. I cut down my strikeouts to 12 in 1923, 21 in 1924, and my average jumped as high as .352.

I reminded Falk that I had seen him play when I was a kid, and recalled a particular incident. The Sox were playing Detroit, and Falk was hitting with two outs in the last of the ninth, one run behind, with the tying run on third. Sylvester Johnson was pitching for Detroit when Falk hit a line drive that hit Johnson on the jaw. The ball rolled to the first baseman, Lu Blue or Johnny Neun, for the third out. "Yeah, I remember that," growled Falk. "It cost me a base hit." It also cost Johnson a broken jaw.

Jim Palmer, perhaps the most successful of any Baltimore pitcher in recent history, offers a pitcher's view. He was quoted in *The Sporting News*: "The secret of effective pitching is to make hitters swing at pitches outside of the strike zone."

Palmer was not necessarily talking about strikeouts. Swinging at pitches out of the strike zone more often results in ineffective contact with the ball and easy outs. Knowing the strike zone is not a natural gift for a player. It is an acquired skill that requires constant discipline, and is best obtained from "adequate minor-league experience." That is the refrain that runs through every manager's commentary, and it's the basis upon which the players of the 1920s and 1930s constructed their careers. That is the dimension that is missing in baseball today.

6 The Minor Leagues, 1920-1949

Although the minor league system existed from the turn of the century, the minor leagues in those early years were loosely organized and not overly aggressive in searching for talent. Most players got their start through a reference from a friend or another player. Often it depended on the initiative of the prospect himself, who would blanket the minors with descriptions of his talent and was lucky to receive a response with an offer of a "tryout." Usually, this meant nothing more than an invitation to camp. If he was accepted, a contract would be offered together with reimbursement for expenses. That was the common procedure. Even the great Ty Cobb had to hustle for merely a "tryout" with a minor club.

In the early 1920s, baseball spread its range of interest throughout the cities and across the countryside of America. The heroics of Babe Ruth dominated sports pages, capturing the imagination of baseball fans, creating new fans, and in the process, inspiring young athletes in the pursuit of baseball as a profession.

Baseball was the predominant sport. It seemed as if every town and hamlet was aspiring to be represented in organized professional baseball. Leagues were regionalized within a state and often combined with those in neighboring states, engendering rivalries among legions of fans. Each league, from class D to AAA, was distinct in character and classification, in quality of play and salaries. The minor leagues were an integral part of the panorama of baseball and a vital source of supply for the major leagues.

If the majors were the body and soul of baseball, the minors were its lifeblood.

In those days, the major leagues operated under player-control limits, as they do today. No major league club was permitted to have, under contract or control, more than a specified number of players. This number varied over the years, running between 30 and 40 players. The practice was to retain what was permitted during seasonal play—20 to 25 players—with the remainder assigned to the minor leagues, under the major league club's control.

Eight or 10 surplus players, however, were not enough for some major league teams, such as the St. Louis Cardinals. They could not compete with the more affluent major league clubs in competition for the purchase of other outstanding minor league players. They could draft players from the minor leagues for a fixed and nominal sum of money, but the best players were in the five highest-ranking minor leagues, whose players were exempt from the major league draft.

Jack Dunn of the Baltimore club knew how to utilize this exemption. He just retained his players until he could command maximum value for them. No one did it any better. Who were some of his players? Babe Ruth, for one. In later years he had Bob Grove, George Earnshaw, Joe Boley and Max Bishop playing at the same time on his Baltimore team. Eventually he sold all four of them to his friend Connie Mack of the Philadelphia Athletics.

What particularly angered many of the major league clubs was that the exempted minor league teams were developing special friendships and connections with particular major league teams, giving preferences to their friends, such as first refusal rights on their minor league talent. The remaining major league clubs claimed they were being shut out of the competition for star players, even if they had the money to compete, which some of them did not have.

As an offset, what was needed and lacking was a method of rounding up young baseball talent and controlling their destiny without violating the major league player-control limits. No longer would there be a need to purchase players from other major league clubs—or from the draft-exempt, high-ranking minor league clubs and their outrageous price tags on their players.

It was an idea whose time had come—and whose grandiosity appealed to the imaginative and fertile brain of Branch Rickey, the general manager of the St. Louis Cardinals. He undertook to establish a system within the system, but outside the shackles of baseball's player-control regulations. Why not "grow" the talent that was needed? Why not a baseball farm?

Rickey had two hurdles to overcome: the acquisition of scouts to locate the young talent, and someplace to put this talent after it was found. The first part was easy. There were many retired, unemployed ex-players with sufficient energy and acumen to cir-culate within assigned territories and spot the major league pros-pects. There would be no signing bonuses for these youngsters. Only stardust in their eyes and visions of reaching the promised land, the major leagues. Once this talent was assembled, they would be culled, graded, and distributed to appropriate levels of competition. They would be moved up or down the ladder in accordance with Rickey's judgment. They would become a con-tinuous source of supply for his St. Louis Cardinals.

The second part, where to place these young prospects, was the bigger problem. But not for long with the innovative Branch Rickey. He established an arrangement of "working agreements" with minor league clubs who were short on talent as well as money. He signed hundreds of good young prospects, whom he then assigned to minor league clubs of his choosing. Rickey re-tained the exclusive right under his working agreements to re-purchase any or all players from these minor league clubs for as little as $100 per player. According to Rickey, these players would not fall within the major league player control limit. To him they were the property of the minor league clubs until such time as he exercised his option to repurchase their contracts.

It didn't take long for the other major league clubs to see the light. In a matter of a year or two, almost every major league club was emulating Rickey's working agreement system. As Leslie O'Connor, former assistant to baseball Commissioner Landis, later testified at a congressional hearing, each club was controlling "at least 200 players." The working agreement led to other abuses. Whenever the opportunity arose, the most ambitious major league clubs acquired ownership interests in the minor league clubs, which they then operated as subsidiaries.

Commissioner Landis knew something about monopolies. He could detect their acrid odor no matter how well it was scented. Landis determined that working agreements were merely a device to circumvent the major league player-control limits. He saw many evils in this practice. The majors were controlling the minor leagues, building huge inventories of players who were languishing in minor league chains at the sole discretion of the parent club. Thus, players were being deterred from "advancing in their chosen profession." He concluded that this practice would destroy the independent minor-league ownerships, inasmuch as no independent owner could compete successfully in the same league with the subsidiary of a major league club. He was determined to put a stop to the insidious practice of chain-store baseball. As a result, Landis ruled that all players controlled by major league clubs under working agreements would fall within the major league player control rule of 40 players per club.

Landis hadn't reckoned with the resourcefulness of the major league operators. They abandoned working agreements in favor of that old standby—gentlemen's agreements. Nothing in writing.

The essence of these verbal agreements was: "You hang on to these players and return them to me when I ask for them."

In due time, players were being shuffled back and forth. As can be expected, disputes broke out between major league clubs and their "unaffiliated" affiliates over title to player contracts. With the tenacious Leslie O'Connor assisting in the groundwork, Landis handed down decision after decision freeing the "slaves." He declared the player a free agent whenever there was the slightest taint of violation of the player-control limits, and he levied a fine against the offending club. These fines, which were paid to covered-up players, amounted to "more than a million dollars in profits to the players concerned," according to Leslie O'Connor. Some of these fortunate beneficiaries were Rick Ferrell, Tommy Henrich, Heinie Manush, Hal McKain, Roy Spencer, Guy Cantrell, Whitey Glazner, Jay Partridge, Ernie Wingard, Claude Jonnard, Mel Simons, Ralph Judd, and Mike McCormick, all of whom eventually became major league players, with varying degrees of success.

The real blow descended upon the Detroit ball club, under the general managership of Jack Zeller. Landis uncovered a mass of Detroit cover-ups. In one sweeping decision he granted free agency to more than one hundred Detroit chattels, virtually denuding that organization of its best minor league talent. Many of these players signed with other major league clubs and received bonuses and lucrative contracts as a result of their freedom. Other players, for technical reasons, were not awarded free agency but received cash awards from the penalized Detroit club. This whopping punishment got the attention of the major league owners, who finally decided to conform to acceptable standards.

Although working agreements were still permitted, it was only on the basis of clearly established, independent ownerships, with the minor league clubs as separate entities. The working-agreement contracts had to be approved by the league offices and the commissioner. No more cover-ups and no gentlemen's agreements.

Thus, when Landis broke up the monopoly game of Branch Rickey and that of other major league clubs, the minor leagues began to flourish again. The draft exemptions previously given to the five minor leagues were removed. All minor league players were now subject to the major league draft, but not until they had served apprenticeships in the minor leagues. These tenures varied, with the higher classifications given the right to retain their players a year or two longer than the lower leagues.

It was in the minors that baseball was taught and learned. Merely advancing a step was a notable accomplishment. Generally, a player started at the bottom and climbed the minor league ladder from one classification to another before reaching the major leagues.

There was no force-feeding of players. They learned to play through competition. For a player, climbing a step in classification meant facing tougher competition—and sometimes falling back— in a continuing quest to reach the top. To become a major league player required a combination of basic ability, the capacity to improve, and the tenacity to endure the hardships of minor league life. This was no easy assignment. Except for a few especially gifted college players—and a sandlotter or two, such as Mel Ott and Jimmie Foxx—a hitch in the minor leagues was a necessity for everyone on their way to the majors. Of the thousands of players who played in the major leagues in the twenties and thirties, only a comparative handful were able to break into the major leagues without minor league experience. Legendary superstars such as Ruth, Cobb, Hornsby, Gehrig, Speaker, Gehringer, Greenberg, Simmons, Cochrane, Hartnett, Dickey, DiMaggio, the Waners, and Ted Williams were minor league trained. Some of baseball's greatest pitchers—Walter Johnson, Dizzy Dean, Bob Grove, and

Dazzy Vance—started their careers in the minors. Obviously, those with better talent made faster progress. Yet three or four years in the minor leagues was not uncommon even for those who eventually reached Hall of Fame status. It would be a safe estimate that 99 percent of the major league players in the 1920s and 1930s, started their careers in the minor leagues.

Hank Greenberg commented on those early days:

> Our attitude toward baseball was different. In the minors we had no outside interests. When traveling, or whenever players got together, we talked baseball. This meant almost all day long. We had time on our hands. We would go to the ball park early and practice such things as running the bases. What foot do we use to hit the bag when making a turn? Outfielders would practice positioning themselves for throws to the bases and to home plate. We enjoyed the experience of learning the strategies of the game. When we reached the majors we knew the fundamentals and were prepared, even though major league competition was much tougher than the minors.

During those years, the minor leagues as well as the majors were at a peak, with exceptional talent waiting for an opportunity to crack a major league roster. There was no schooling in the major leagues. Once a player put on a major league uniform, he was expected to know how to play the game. There were no coaches to straighten out a batting or pitching flaw or to counsel a player in critical game situations. A player had to know the fundamentals of the game from the moment he joined a major league roster.

There was no waiting for an aspiring major league player to prove himself. If a Joe Cronin didn't quickly impress the Pittsburgh club, it was back to the minors for him. Pitchers such as Burleigh Grimes, Jess Haines, Carl Hubbell, and Dazzy Vance were rejected by their original major-league clubs. These men are now Hall of Famers. Many other exceptional players who didn't stick in the majors in their first year or two were returned to the minors, eventually finding their way back for long and successful major-league careers.

The Depression years in the 1930s were a particularly trying time for the players, whether in the major or minor leagues. Many minor leagues quit operations in the 1930s, the number of active leagues falling to a low of fourteen in 1933. The major leagues cut down both in the size of their rosters and their payrolls. Many players took cuts in salary. Players of major league quality were returned to the minors. There was more talent available to the majors and the minors than what could be used.

There is no way of estimating how many players have been lost to baseball, players who could have become major leaguers but for the lack of discovery and opportunity. As Billy Herman said, the kid who was hurt was the one who had potential but couldn't find a place to play.

I know what Billy Herman was talking about. I can cite an example based upon personal knowledge. When in high school, my brother Dave was an exceptionally talented baseball player. He was the subject of an article in the *Chicago Tribune* that rated him as probably the best baseball player in the Chicago city high schools. He was only 18 years old.

His outfielding style was patterned after Tris Speaker. Dave would "receive" fly balls two-handed, as Speaker did, hands cupped and held high, almost at the chin. The advantage in that style was being able to throw without wasted motion.

Based upon the current method of rating baseball prospects, Dave would have qualified in every phase of play. One can imagine the attention a high school player would get today with Dave's credentials. Yet not a single scout, or anyone else in baseball, made any overture to Dave. He was totally overlooked.

Even the lowly class-D leagues were tough to crack. I can speak with some authority about what class-D baseball was like in 1931, when I broke in with Lincoln in the Nebraska State League. The minor leagues today are a paradise compared to those in earlier days. We had no clubhouse, no trainers, no traveling instructors to work with us, and no parent club to watch over us. Our contracts were standard—$75.00 per month, subject to termination on 1 day's notice. If injured, it was 10 days' notice and a release. Our contracts bound us in perpetuity to the club. This was a comforting feeling, not a burden. If they kept us, it meant we had some ability, our jobs were secure, and we could nourish the hope of being sold to a higher-ranking team.

Our greatest concern was to avoid a release. We couldn't afford to get out of the lineup even for an injury, let alone for a batting slump or any other playing deficiency. The owners were impatient with injured players. I recall breaking a little finger while catching. It was put into a splint—tied to the adjoining finger—and I played. Stepping out of the lineup with an injury was inviting the loss of your job. The stands contained not only the hometown fans, but also ball players recently released from higher-ranking leagues. They were waiting to replace some player on the field. Those of us in uniform were well aware of them and in a way we envied them. They had some place to go, to class D. But where does a class-D player go if he doesn't cut it? If there was any latent talent in us, it surfaced quickly. For us in class D, there was no turning back—no bridges for retreat. None of us talked of reaching the majors. Our objective was survival, to hold our jobs, and if good enough, to advance the next year to class C or B.

The Lincoln ball park looked like a combat zone—no grass— with dilapidated stands and equipment. Our games were played at night, under a lighting system that consisted of basins, resembling washtubs, which were stationed on the roofs of the low stands. Each tub held three open incandescent lamps, many of which flickered through our games as if in the death throes of their fading lives. The players often commented that the ideal type of baseball cap would be one that was designed like a miner's cap, with an illuminated peak. The night lighting, such as it was, attracted swarms of large flying beetles who punctuated our games with sounds of small explosions when they made contact with the overheated lamps.

All baseballs, however battered and soiled, were preserved by the owners, who had a simple method of cleaning them: they dipped them in whitewash. Eventually, these whitewashed balls were put into games and came at the hitters with no visible seams. It was like hitting at a cue ball in virtual darkness. It scared hell out of us.

I remember the night that Al Benton joined our club in midseason. He arrived with a wardrobe consisting of two articles of clothing—sandals and bib overalls. Benton subsequently became a pretty good major league pitcher and even pitched for my San Diego Pacific Coast League team in later years.

In Lincoln he was a big, awkward, rawboned guy who could throw a sponge through a brick wall. His first appearance was in relief, and his first warmup pitch nearly undressed me. My glove and the sponge inside my mitt went flying in different directions. In those days catchers warmed up pitchers without wearing the face mask. I couldn't get to my mask fast enough. When Benton was finally ready to pitch to his first hitter, I backed up about three feet, in tandem with the umpire, got down on one knee, and awaited whatever the fates had in store for me. But no hitter approached the plate.

Now no one has yet found a way to play a baseball game without a hitter somewhere in the vicinity of the batter's box. It seemed that the scheduled hitter had a problem. In calculating the factors of hitting against a wild, overpowering pitcher who was throwing a seamless baseball in the dark, he apparently came to ponder some basic metaphysical questions: How much is my life worth? Who will take care of the farm after I'm gone? There was nothing the opposing manager could do the persuade that hitter to take a chance with his destiny.

Eventually a reluctant, substitute hitter was produced, and the game continued. I believe the story about the rookie who faced Walter Johnson for the first time, when Johnson was in his prime. The batter took two quick strikes and headed for the dugout, instructing the umpire to keep the third strike—he had seen enough. Against Benton that night, the hitters conceded *before* they reached the plate. A benevolent Providence interceded. Benton suddenly complained of a soreness in his arm and was removed from the game—to the relief of the hitters and, especially me.

In those days we dressed in boarding houses when at "home," and walked to the ball park. For road games we traveled by a vehicle that was called a "bus"—but resembled a rickety crate attached to wheels that were not necessarily round or coordinated. We traveled at night, piling into the "bus" after our last home game, often wearing our uniforms as we took off on long rides to such places as McCook, Grand Island, North Platte, and Norfolk.

The problem with the night trips was the cold air that poured through the broken isinglass windows. I don't remember ever being warm enough. Often we would arrive at daybreak barely in time to check into what was euphemistically called a hotel, snatch a few hours of sleep, wolf a quick breakfast, and then head to the ball park for an afternoon game.

Ball players today don't know what playing in the heat is like if they've never played under the midsummer sun in North Platte, Nebraska. We sat on open benches with not a semblance of shade for the players. There was not a blade of grass, only sandy soil so hot that the rivets on the inside of our spiked shoes burned our feet. We found relief by sticking our feet, shoes and all, into buckets of water. We used a similar strategy at night to overcome the intense heat in our rooms—pouring a pitcher or two of water directly on the bed, where we would flop, cool off, and eventually manage a tortured sleep.

Above all, we learned how to play baseball. Our manager was Les Nunamaker, an old-time, no-nonsense ex–major leaguer. Our conversations were always baseball talk. Every morning, following a night game, we'd assemble at the ball park for strategy sessions. This consisted of reviews of the previous game and analyses of our mistakes. No compliment was ever offered for making a good play. It was Nunamaker's philosophy that performing well is "what you're paid to do." From our fixed $75.00-per-month salaries, we had to supply our own bats, as well as pay for all of our "home" expenses. Yet we managed to save a few dollars to get home after the season.

We were happy to have made good in professional baseball.

From the time that Judge Landis laid down his decisions that effectively controlled the voracity of the major leagues, the minor leagues began to expand and prosper. These leagues were independently owned and operated almost entirely by people with previous professional baseball experience. They were able to judge talent, and their appraisals of the players on their minor league clubs and on others were respected by the major league teams.

What was lacking in gate receipts was substantially offset by the sale of a player or two. Some clubs, such as our San Diego Pacific Coast League operation, had their own small but effective farm system. We employed scouts and we competed favorably with the majors for talented local high-school players.

Jack Harshman, for example, was a high school player that we acquired by outbidding major league clubs for his services. How did we do it? We offered and subsequently paid Harshman a percentage of his sales price. The sale of his contract to the

New York Giants involved a substantial sum of cash plus three players, including Jack Graham, who became a superstar for us in the Pacific Coast League. We were successful in signing Floyd Robinson to his first contract, subsequently selling his contract to the White Sox, where he enjoyed a successful career. We acquired Tom Alston, whom we sold to the Cardinals for the largest price ever paid for a minor league player in baseball's history. The players we received in that transaction brought us a Pacific Coast League championship the following year. We were not alone in such experiences. The majors and the minors had a well-developed system that profited both organizations.

In 1949 the minor leagues operated and survived under the protection of the Major-Minor League Agreement, which granted exclusive territorial rights to minor league clubs. These rights covered an area of 75 miles surrounding the base of a club. That provision was especially vital to the existence of the Pacific Coast League. The Los Angeles and San Francisco territories, which represented the heart of the Coast League, were coveted by certain major league owners. The Major-Minor League Agreement did not prohibit any major league club from taking Los Angeles or San Francisco, or any other minor league city. It was permitted, but not without "just compensation." That would have been a difficult issue to resolve and most likely would have ended up in the courts, with the potential of huge damage awards to the Pacific Coast League clubs.

The territorial rights provision also protected and enabled us to restrict the competing transmission into our minor league territories of major league radio and television broadcasts in competition with our own. That was no small matter. Radio and television rights represented big money in those days for the Pacific Coast League. For example, our San Diego club was receiving $60,000 for the radio broadcasting rights of our games. This was especially important money that was not shared with the visiting clubs or with the league office. It represented whole dollars to us, the equivalent of 150,000 gate admissions.

In 1949, baseball commissioner "Happy" Chandler issued an edict declaring the territorial rights provision in the Major-Minor League Agreement null and void. That egregious decision set off shock waves in the Pacific Coast League and presaged the doom of the minor leagues.

The effects were immediate. The floodgates were opened for the saturation of major league broadcasts—radio and television—into minor league territories. The $60,000 fee for our San Diego broadcasting rights fell to $10,000 in one year. Our choice Pacific Coast League cities were now available to major league owners without the payment of huge damages. There was no feasible way our clubs could prevent their takeover, nor did we have any leverage to participate in its benefits. The path was now clear for Walter O'Malley to plan his move to Los Angeles.

Chandler did have some problems that led him into his decision. Organized baseball was under attack from Congress over its special exemption from the antitrust laws. A Congressional committee was threatening to use its power to remove that exemption, thus imperiling the reserve clause, the foundation of baseball's structure. It was apparent that the restraints on the dissemination of major league telecasts into minor league territories, which were imposed by the territorial rights clause, were not in the public interest and no longer defendable.

Chandler had the duty to try to preserve baseball's exemption under the antitrust laws, even at the sacrifice of the territorial protection of the minor leagues. Chandler also had the duty to protect the minor leagues from the consequences of his decision.

He could have considered the loss of revenues to all the minor league clubs by the transmission of major league games into their territories. He could have required that the minor leagues be given a participating share in the *extra* monies the major league clubs would be receiving for the inclusion of the minor league territories into the major league radio and television networks. Chandler's decision enriched the majors at the expense of the minors. For the minor leagues, there was simply not enough revenue from gate admissions to keep them financially solvent. Thus, some participation in the new monies could have kept the minors in business. Further, the prospect of future increases in these revenues would have made the minor league franchises more valuable and would have helped stabilize the minor league system.

At the time of the Chandler decision in 1949, the minors had a high of 59 leagues. Those 59 leagues bracketed over 400 cities in the United States and Canada, with more than 6,500 players in the system. Today the 17 minor leagues include 3 Rookie Leagues and the Mexican League, which were not part of organized baseball in 1949. These leagues are scattered over several countries, with dubious classifications. Only a small percentage of these players are major league prospects. The majority of players are on the minor league rosters only for the purpose of providing the younger prospects an opportunity to play in game competition.

These leagues are often subsidized by the majors, sometimes with two major league clubs splitting the cost of sponsoring one minor league team. With the expansion of the major leagues, from 16 to 26 teams, there has been a shortage of major league talent to fill their needs. Thus, young, inexperienced players are prematurely placed on major league rosters—without adequate exposure to top-level minor league competition and without sufficient knowledge of many vital fundamentals of baseball.

There is not a major league manager who will deny the need for more minor league experience for the young players. This gap is a sore spot with them, and their most common complaint.

The system has gone into reverse. Instead of players developing in an established, independently owned minor league system, with the minors bearing the operating costs, the financial burden is now on the major leagues. Doubts are developing among major league owners about the value and even the necessity of the minor leagues. The minor leagues do not serve the same purpose as in the early days in baseball. Some owners are beguiled with the direct route of college football and basketball players to the top professional ranks. But baseball is different. To reach the major leagues requires adequate minor league experience. With rare exceptions, this also applies to the best college players. Considering the current decimated minor-league system, where can players get the necessary experience?

How different it might have been but for an unfortunate decision in 1949.

7 Attitudes in the 1920s and 1930s

Baseball in the 1920s and 1930s was played under restrictive conditions that do not exist today. In many of those early years, for example, the team rosters were smaller and, of necessity, limited to complete players. This meant that players had to have the ability to hit effectively against left- and right-handed pitching and to play competently at their defensive positions as well. There was no room on those rosters for one-dimensional players such as Smead Jolley, Zeke Bonura, Ike Boone, and Buzz Arlett. Solid players, many in their prime years, were bandied about in trades or cash sales almost by impulse. The impatience of the trigger-happy owners in those days was the hallmark of their operations.

It was Branch Rickey's theory that it was better to dispose of a player one year too soon than one year too late, an excellent theory with excellent results for Rickey. He had minor league subsidiaries second to none, with numerous "phenoms" available for every position. But it did not work that well with many other clubs, which didn't have Rickey's backup system.

One "off-year" by a player was often enough to propel a club owner into trade or sale negotiations. An off-year could have been nothing more than a modest drop-off in hitting from the previous year. Wally Berger talked about being traded to the New York Giants:

I'm not sure why the Braves disposed of me after the 1936 season. I was only 31 years old. I had a pretty good year, hitting .288, with 25 home runs and 91 runs batted in. Not as good as the year before, when I led the league in two categories, 34 homers and 130 runs batted in. And I considered myself a pretty decent outfielder.

What salary would a player command today if he could accomplish what Berger did in his "mediocre" year?

Hank Greenberg recalled:

It was hard to break into a major league lineup during my time. The lineups of the major league clubs were set with complete players. Yet one bad year for a major leaguer and the owners assumed that the player was on the way down. There were no multiyear contracts to protect a player's job or his salary. Great players, such as Gehrig, had to take a salary cut if they fell off a little from one year to another. It happened to me, too. I understand even DiMaggio was asked to take a cut in salary while in his prime. As a result of only one off-year—and it needn't be a totally bad year—many outstanding players were traded or sold.

In discussing this phase of baseball with Buzzie Bavasi, a prominent baseball executive for many years, I displayed a list of players, including subsequent Hall of Famers, who were traded or sold in the 1920s or 1930s. Many of these players were comparatively young at the time, some in their twenties. After studying the list, Bavasi expressed his dismay: "Players of that quality would never be traded today. What amazes me is why anyone would trade or sell off those catchers. That's the hardest commodity to replace."

The list of catchers included Al Lopez, Gus Mancuso, Spud Davis, Bob O'Farrell, Luke Sewell, Muddy Ruel, Rick Ferrell, Rollie Hemsley, Jimmie Wilson, Frankie Pytlak, and even Mickey Cochrane. "Today," said Bavasi, "it would be unthinkable."

I then showed Bavasi another list of players. I asked, "Could these players have played in the majors today?"

That list included non–Hall of Famers Babe Herman, Augie Galan, Ival Goodman, Hank Leiber, Dolf Camilli, Wally Berger,

Lonny Frey, Phil Cavarretta, Frank Demaree, Johnny Hopp, Stan Hack, Woody Jensen, Dick Bartell, Marv Owen, Frankie Crosetti, Ben Chapman, Hal Trosky, Willie Kamm, Gus Suhr, and Terry Moore. Bavasi pondered the list and said: "If I had a lineup in my last 10 years with players of that ability, I would have won a pennant every year with no sweat."

For better or worse, many changes that are now an integral part of the game weren't dreamed of in the 1920s and 1930s. Who could have predicted totally enclosed, air-conditioned stadiums? Or artificial turf and designated hitters? Platooning was infrequent, and the "role" player was unheard of. The better teams maintained a set lineup year after year. Player rosters today comprise 24 players for each club, plus whatever players can be added by judicious use of the disabled list. The complete player and the set lineup are rare today.

Sparky Anderson made this point about set lineups:

> Platooning is an advantage. Two players of equal ability—one a left-handed hitter and the other a right-handed hitter—are more effective than one player. It keeps more players in the game. It gives me a player in reserve. I can get better results from a combination of two players—not tired—than what would be possible from one tired player.

There is merit in Anderson's views. The larger number of players on a roster, the greater the need to keep them active and content. Yet it is hard to escape the value of complete players who can play effectively, day after day, against all types of pitching. The problem today lies with the inability of many left-handed hitters coping with left-handed pitching. Thus, platooning with right-handed hitters is a necessity for major league clubs today.

In an interview I had with Ossie Bluege, he said:

> The rosters of the early 1920s and 1930s were limited. There just wasn't room for the extra players that are carried on major league rosters today. You had to be a complete player to nail down a spot. Players had to

hit left- and right-handed pitching. Of course a left-handed hitter preferred to face right-handed pitching. But he didn't have any choice. We played every day, facing all types of pitchers.

Glenn Wright was a superstar shortstop with Pittsburgh and Brooklyn in the twenties. Shortly before his death in 1984, I conducted an interview with him. He was bedridden at the time. I composed a series of questions, which he answered through his son. To one of the questions—"How would you compare baseball today with the way it was played during your time?"—he responded:

> It was better in the 1920s and 1930s. The players today are bigger, stronger, and somewhat faster, and play with better equipment and on better fields. But somehow, for the most part they don't play as well. Perhaps this is due to a lack of intensity, mental toughness—or their attitude toward the game.

The dedication of the players that Glenn Wright stressed could very well have been induced by the players' insecurities during the Depression years. In the 1920s and 1930s, players played with injuries, always afraid that once out of the lineup they might not regain their positions. For the majority of players, an injury such as a broken leg or a beaning usually meant the end of their major league careers or rehabilitation in the minors. Only the superstars could survive a disabling injury with any reasonable assurance of reclaiming their place in the lineup. As Willie Kamm put it:

> Players were expected to play with injuries. Players who were beaned rarely regained their hitting ability. They seemed to be permanently damaged and didn't last long. But those were the chances you took in playing baseball in those days. It was a constant battle just to survive.

The adverse conditions that the early-day players faced were incentives that pushed them to perform to the maximum of their potential. They had no alternative but to dedicate themselves to baseball. It represented their entire livelihood. There was no big money for them to set aside for their future, for investments, or for secondary careers. There were no pensions to look forward to. For almost all of these players, it was a month-to-month existence.

Hank Greenberg commented on the attitudes of the players during his time: "If I went one game without hitting the ball well, I would be taking extra batting practice the next day. This wasn't anything unusual. Lou Gehrig followed that routine, as did many other good hitters."

Another aspect of the style of baseball in the 1920s and 1930s was the strict professionalism of the players. Nothing offended the old-timers more than showboating, hotdogging, or a player trying to "show up" an opposing player or team. The prevailing attitude was: Don't antagonize the opposition. Let sleeping dogs lie.

Modern-day players have a similar attitude about not demeaning their contemporaries. They too deplore unprofessional conduct. But the game has changed, and in the process some of that professionalism has become tarnished. In the twenties and thirties, there was no waiting around at home plate watching a home run disappear into the stands; no walking around the bases on a home run in lieu of the customary trot; no encores; and no high fives.

In those earlier years, a stolen base was a highly regarded achievement in a close game but strictly taboo when meaningless to the game's outcome. This attitude also prevailed in the 1940s and 1950s. Bob Lemon said: "If any player stole a base on me with his side having a big lead, the next time that player would come to the plate, he'd be on his back with the first pitch. We did not appreciate any player trying to show us up."

Although the old-timers were well aware of their own statistics, it was a subject that was never openly discussed. Today nothing is sacred or confidential. Individual statistics and salaries are everyday topics of conversation among the players.

Baseball players today go public in criticism of their team-mates, their managers, their owners, and even the cities they play in. In turn, managers and owners vent public criticism of their players. If a player wants to be traded, he tells the media about it, and the owner responds in kind. In comparison, the players of the 1920s and 1930s were mute. Public criticism by them was a rarity, exercised only by the superstars, sometimes to their regret.

Frankie Frisch once commented on the trade in 1927 that sent him from the New York Giants to the St. Louis Cardinals in exchange for Rogers Hornsby: "I talked back to McGraw, which nobody was supposed to do. That brought me a ticket to St. Louis." Of course, manager McGraw didn't exactly get a shrinking violet in Hornsby. What made that trade significant was that it involved the best player on each of those clubs. Even superstars were not sacrosanct.

Travel conditions were also different in the 1920s and 1930s. Writers and players today often cite the burdens of plane travel and the jet lag that players supposedly endure. Jet lag? The longest flight, coast to coast, is a four-and-a-half- to five-hour affair. The plane accommodations today are choice—in wide-body jets and air-conditioned comfort. By the time the players are settled, fed, and relaxed by a nap, the flight is over. Upon arrival at their desti-nation, they are transported to first-class hotels, where at least eight hours of sleep is available to them before heading for the ball park.

The current-day plane trips would have been joy rides to the old-timers of the twenties and thirties. In those early days, major league baseball was confined between the East Coast and the Mississippi River. A train ride from St. Louis or Chicago to Boston or New York was a 24-hour overnight affair in cinder-polluted trains over corrugated road beds. Air-conditioning was unknown. Opening a window was a hazard that covered the passengers with grime. Sleeping accommodations were in virtually airless berths, featuring a lower and an upper bunk bed, with drapes to conceal the occupants. There were no amenities such as closets, only a net, attached to the inside of the berth, to hold one's apparel for the overnight ride. It required a remarkable constitution for a player to sleep in those berths. The lower berths were the preferred accommodations, being slightly wider and with a window to provide some distraction. These lowers were assigned to the regular players and often to the pitcher scheduled for the next game. The upper berths were hardly more than a coop, just big enough to hold an average-sized player—with no windows, no air, no sleep.

Jigger Statz saw some value in the train rides:

> It's true that the trains were uncomfortable, yet I enjoyed the spare time we had on those long rides. The players would talk baseball, and we would even plan special plays. On one of these trips I worked out a play with our infielders on the Cubs. It applied only to a special situation, runners on first and second with less than two outs. On a short fly to center the runners would naturally hold their bases. I would then deliberately trap the ball and then toss it to the infielder, who would first tag the runner on second and then touch the base for a double play. A ball caught by an outfielder is not an infield fly. So the infielders would back away from the ball and let me take it. Once in a while the infielder would make the mistake of first touching the base and then the runner, and we would lose the double play. It's such an easy maneuver, although I never see it today.

Today there is more of a laid-back attitude in baseball. Willie Stargell echoed that sentiment when he returned to the Pittsburgh Pirates as a coach in June or 1985: "I just hope I don't give the wrong sign out there at first base. It's just a case of having fun again, and that's what the game is all about. I just want to get down there and see that the guys have some fun."

If "fun" is synonymous with enjoying one's work, then no one can dispute Stargell's approach. Unfortunately, "fun" in baseball today often takes on the characteristics of horsing around on the bench, eating, and not paying attention to what is transpiring on the ball field. That type of "fun" comes easier to players whose futures are secured by long-term contracts. To the players of the twenties and thirties, baseball was a comparatively serious business. On the bench there was no such thing as "fun." Idle conversation, horsing around, or inattention to the activities on the ball field were taboos. The demeanor of the players was grim and intense.

The intensity emphasized by Glenn Wright sometimes showed up in strange ways. Earl Whitehill was one of the baseball's premier pitchers in the 1920s and 1930s. He was a firebrand when pitching, aptly described in the terminology of those days as a "red-ass." I recall his parading up and down the Washington dugout, berating the players for not producing runs. He demanded production. Nobody quarreled with him. They understood his intensity, his keen winning spirit.

I had a personal experience with Whitehill that was indicative of his attitude. I was assigned as his catcher in a game in Boston. Whitehill had his own set of signs for his catchers to use. In the first inning, I had difficulty in communicating those signs to him. Pretty soon he was stomping around the rubber, his hands in the air—as if bemoaning, "Look what I have to work with."

I walked out to him, nervously, and admitted, "I'm having trouble with your signs. Would you instead go along with my set of signs?"

"What in hell are your signs?"

I explained what I had in mind and he agreed to try it. We

worked a twelve-inning game, beating Boston, 3 to 2. I was able to throw out three Red Sox runners in that game. Billy Werber, the American League's leading base-stealer was thrown out only seven times that year. I got him twice in that game.

When the game was over, Whitehill came to me with a pat on the back, a big handshake, and an invitation to join him for dinner. As I sat across him at the dinner table, I found him to be one of the most affable, mildest persons I'd met. We became friends. But when he was pitching, he was nobody's friend—not even with the players on his own team.

Every major league club had their share of Whitehills—intense, determined, all-out players, totally dedicated, as Glenn Wright described. That dedication was as dominant in hitting as it was in pitching, and was in later years exemplified by Ralph Kiner. I asked him how he accounted for the reduction from his league-leading 109 strikeouts in 1946 to a more modest 81 strikeouts the next year.

Kiner responded:

It was Hank Greenberg's influence, when he came to Pittsburgh in 1947. His career was mostly in the thirties and apparently his baseball attitudes were shaped in those years. He impressed several principles on me. He showed me the sense of standing closer to the plate. That immediately made it tougher on the pitchers. In effect, I reduced their strike zone. He insisted that I know my particular hitting zone. And above all, practice, practice, practice.

Hank Greenberg commented:

Ralph was an apt pupil. He caught on quick. I gave him some calculations to consider: "Suppose you play 150 games and average 4 times at bat. That's roughly 600 times at bat, totaling about 2,400 pitches. Suppose 1,000 of those were strikes. Do you think you could hit 35 of those strikes out of the park?" Ralph said, "Of course." That thought stayed with him. He looked for strikes. He hit 51 homers that year against 23 the year before. His batting average jumped from .246 to .313.

Ralph Kiner acquired from Greenberg the characteristics of baseball as it was played in the twenties and thirties—determination and dedication.

8 Knockdowns, Brushbacks, and Pitching

"You #%'$&/, you've been hitting me pretty good. You're going down on your ass today."*
—A message from Dizzy Dean, exponent of the high-neck-in pitch

It has often been said that hitting a baseball is the single most difficult act in all sports. If you've never played professional baseball , you will better understand what hitting is about by marking off a distance of 60 feet 6 inches, the span between the pitching slab and home plate, and then stepping into an imaginary batter's box. Your first reaction will be a surprising awareness of how short this distance really is. Then visualize a pitcher's mound, approximately 10 inches high, from which a pitcher, 6 feet tall or more, takes a giant step toward the plate and delivers a fast-moving baseball. The release point of the pitch can shorten the distance to the plate by as much as 6 feet. The pitch might be a fastball, traveling over 90 miles per hour. Or it might be a "breaking" ball, such as a curve, a slider, a split-finger sinker, a screwball, or even a "spitter," each of which moves in a different direction.

Often a pitch is directed close to a hitter, under his chin. Perhaps it's unintentional, but intimidating and dangerous nevertheless.

In the twenties and thirties, the hitters were vulnerable at all times. A nothing-and-two count on a hitter automatically called for a high inside pitch. Many managers would fine a pitcher who permitted a batter to get a base hit on a no-ball–two-strike count. Thus brushbacks and even knockdowns were routine in such situations, a part of the pitcher's arsenal and a part of the game that both sides understood, utilized, and accepted. The idea was not to hit the batter but to intimidate him.

Some pitchers would not throw at hitters. I remember Herman "Old Folks" Pillette, a teammate of mine on the 1937 San Diego Padres in the Pacific Coast League. At that time, Herman was finishing a pitching career of more than 20 years in the Pacific Coast League, in addition to a couple of good years with Detroit when Ty Cobb was manager.

Herman was an extremely friendly guy with a cheerful disposition and a constant smile that often erupted into roars of laughter. He had some interesting theories about pitching. He believed that every pitcher had a limited number of pitches in his arm and that the life span of the arm was reduced with each throw. Therefore, he refused to waste a pitch by throwing at hitters. This was appreciated by the managers and players on the other teams, who in turn tolerated Pillette's tendency to cheat now and then when he was pitching.

Only on special occasions would Pillette throw at a hitter, such as when instructed to put a hitter on base with an intentional walk. Pillette couldn't see any benefit in wasting three extra pitches. Instead, he would take dead aim at the hitter and park one in his ribs. Whenever Pillette was told to give a hitter an intentional walk, I could see the hitter blanch and start moving out of the box. It didn't help. Herman would find him. Occasionally hitters would call out to Herman, "Not too hard," and Herman would good naturedly oblige.

One afternoon when I was sitting alongside of Pillette on a long train ride to the Northwest, I suggested a pitching strategy to him. "Instead of hitting the batter on an intentional walk," I said, "why don't you slip a strike across the plate and get ahead of him in the count."

Herman seemed offended. "I can't do that," he said. "I've been pitching this way for years. They know I won't cross them up. So they don't complain when I load up the ball once in a while and throw them a wet one."

I remember one of those "wet ones." I was trying to throw out a runner stealing second base. The ball slithered out of my hand and was retrieved by the right fielder. I told Herman, "I can handle spit on a ball but not a booger."

"I know," he said. "It's happened to other catchers too."

In view of the tolerance shown him, Herman felt it would be deceitful to cross up a hitter by throwing a strike across the plate while the hitter, anticipating being hit by the pitch, was leaning out of the box. I regretted my treacherous suggestion. It was dishonest of me to ask Pillete to violate his standard of honest dishonesty.

Brushback pitches do no harm. It's the knockdown pitch, a pitch at the batter's shoulders, that is dangerous. It's the rare pitcher who will use the batter's shoulders for a target. In 1960 Branch Rickey commented on this phase of baseball in his book, *The American Diamond*:

> The high inside pitch is a "purpose" pitch. It is the strikeout pitch of all ages. . . . But I don't think there is a pitcher in all of baseball who would deliberately throw at a batter's head with the full intention of hitting him in the head. Furthermore, no one in the history of baseball has been hit on the head by a pitch that was thrown as high as the batter's head. A batter lowers his head when he takes his [batting] stride. The Carl May's pitch that hit and killed Chapman was chest high.

Occasionally a player would get hit by an errant pitch. It could hurt like hell—but he didn't rub. Why give the impression that the pitcher accomplished anything? He didn't complain, and above all he never charged the mound, precipitating a fight that might involve both benches. Players of the 1920s and 1930s saw the situation differently from the way players do today. They felt a complaint indicated that they could be intimidated by inside pitches—and from then on they would be facing a steady diet of pitches that were "high and tight." Fights would break out occasionally between a pitcher and a hitter over a verbal challenge and would sometimes involve other players—but rarely because of a brushback or knockdown pitch.

The modern-day player has a different view of such pitches. He sees brushback pitches and even unintentional knockdown pitches as a challenge to his manhood. He feels he will lose the respect of his teammates unless he seeks redress by charging the mound and throwing punches at the pitcher. These confrontations often bring both benches into action, and invariably some players get hurt—and not necessarily the original combatants.

If hit by a pitch or knocked down, some players would retaliate in other ways. Willie Kamm describes an experience involving Ty Cobb:

> I thought Cobb was a friend of mine. Well, maybe not a friend—but friendlier to me than with most other players. Yet that didn't stop him from sliding into me at third one day, spikes high. I got exactly 10 cuts on my leg on that play, mostly nicks—but a few required some patching. Our pitcher was Red Faber, a pretty tough customer himself. When Cobb came up to hit, Faber knocked him down—on his back. The next pitch was the same— down goes Cobb. He didn't say anything. The third pitch was another knockdown. You could see the anger in Cobb's face. With the count now 3 and 0, Faber laid the pitch over the plate. Cobb dragged a bunt to Bud Clancy, our first baseman. That situation calls for the pitcher to cover first, but Faber never left the mound. Can't blame him. Cobb would have cut his legs off him.

With full awareness of brushacks and knockdowns, the old-timers still crowded the plate. In a one-run type of a game, getting on base was an imperative, even if it meant deliberately getting hit with a pitch. Ossie Bluege rated Bucky Harris as a master at that technique: "He wore those long, loose sleeves, and extended his arms over the plate. Anything close, and he would turn his arm, actually his sleeve, into the pitch. Don't recall his ever getting hurt. But it was a dangerous practice."

In the twenties and thirties, as well as in the forties and fifties, a high inside pitch, a knockdown pitch, was automatically delivered following a home run. The target was the next hitter, who, of course, was innocent of the offense of homering. The hitters understood the pitcher's anger and accepted the "high-neck-in" pitch, as Dizzy Dean labeled it. Thus the pitcher discharged his wrath and salvaged his pride with a high inside pitch to the next hitter, and the game continued.

Babe Herman described his experience with knockdown pitches:

> Whenever someone hit a home run in a tight game, it was certain that the next hitter was going to be dropped. That never bothered me when I was the next hitter. I was ready for the knockdown, even putting on a little extra flourish as I went down, to make the pitcher believe that he really gave me the works. Where it helped me was that I knew that was the end of the knockdowns for me. Now I could really dig in. In those situations, it was just one knockdown that didn't hit the batter—it just dirtied his uniform a little.

The value of knockdown pitches is questionable. Although the threat of a knockdown pitch can keep a hitter from digging in at the plate, such pitches often boomerang.

I recall a knockdown experience on the Albany club of the International League in 1935. I was catching a game against Newark, which had Ernie Koy on their roster, a player of Indian heritage, appropriately called "Chief." His fierce look was enough to rally the troops and start circling the wagons. He was big, a college fullback with sprinter's speed, and a tough hitter at the plate. Our manager was Al Mamaux, whose specialties were displaying his singing voice on any occasion and conducting a daily meeting before each game.

In discussing Koy during a meeting, he told John Rigney, who was to pitch that day: "Don't be afraid to knock him down. When you throw at him, he'll go berserk, maybe out of control. But he will lose his concentration and you'll get him out." Sounded good to me.

The first time, I called for a knockdown pitch which Rigney threw behind Koy's head. That's the surest message of a knockdown that a hitter can get. But Koy ignored the pitch and didn't say a word. The next pitch he hit between the outfielders and breezed into third with a triple. OK, we'll get him the next time.

His second time at bat brought a pitch at his noggin, which he avoided by a mere bob of his head. Again, not a word. This guy was really stoic. He converted Rigney's second pitch into another drive between the outfielders, another triple. Except— *what's this?* Koy is not stopping at third. He's now in high gear headed for the plate—and for *me!* I had the ball in time when he hit me. He rode me like a sled, partway to the stands. I don't recall if I held the ball or not. It didn't matter. All I could think of was Mamaux and his goddamned knockdown pitches.

It is never good strategy to throw at an opposing hitter who is in a batting slump. Even a poor hitter becomes tougher when challenged. A better tactic that the old-timers used was to commiserate with such a hitter, offering him sympathy for his predicament, a not so subtle reminder of his problem that tended to keep him mired in his depression. That precept also applied to a ball club that was not going well. You never agitated a player or a team that was going poorly.

A new rule is being tested in 1988. The umpires are now authorized to eject a pitcher and even his manager if a mere brushback pitch is presumed to be a retaliatory pitch in an argument between the clubs.

As long as baseball has been played, the high inside pitch has been part of a basic pitching strategy. It sets up a hitter for the low outside pitch. The brushback pitch is intended to keep a hitter from leaning into the ball and a bit nervous. Under the new 1988 regulations, umpires will require clairvoyance to read a pitcher's mind. Was it a retaliatory pitch or a routine part of pitching strategy?

If the purpose of the new brushback rule is to put a stop to the melees between clubs over brushback and knockdown pitches, there is a better way to correct this problem. Any player who charges the mound, for whatever reason, should be immediately ejected and fined. If the player is a second offender, he should be more heavily fined and suspended. This approach may produce more brushbacks, more intimidation, and even a few knockdowns, but not necessarily more hit batsmen or injuries. Baseball was never a game for the fainthearted.

To a man, the old-timers approve of the batting helmet and regret that these helmets were not available to them. Chalk up another accolade for Branch Rickey, the progenitor of the batting helmet. Although ridiculed at first, the batting helmet has become an accepted and necessary protective device in baseball. There isn't a player, old-timer or new-timer, who doesn't agree on the value of the batting helmet. What is puzzling, however, is why batting averages haven't improved with the adoption of the helmet. Certainly the helmet provides a hitter with a little more confidence at the plate. Wally Berger said:

> The batting helmet is a great idea. Sure wish we had it when I was playing. I was beaned four times in Portland, the year before I came up to the majors. Luckily they were glancing blows and didn't affect me. In those days, you were always getting high inside pitches when the count was against you. The batting helmet would have made me more comfortable at the plate and would have helped my hitting, and others too.

Aside from knockdown and brushback pitches, the style of pitching was different in the twenties and thirties. The modern-day starting pitcher can go all out, fully aware that a fresh arm is in the bullpen, ready to replace him. The teams in those early years couldn't afford the luxury of that extra arm. Their smaller pitching staffs compelled their starting pitchers to pace themselves and finish the game. It was the starting pitcher's responsibility to win or lose. That may have been necessary in the early days, but not today, when each club carries at least a 10-man pitching staff. With the longer schedule and the championship series, an extra pitcher or two on current-day rosters is justified. Today, every club isolates a crew of relief pitchers, "long" men, "middle-inning" men, and "short" men. They are vital elements in modern-day baseball. Some have received Most Valuable Player awards, an unheard-of honor for a relief pitcher in previous years. Their importance today can be evidenced by their salaries, which are among the highest on their clubs.

In the 1920s and 1930s, a pitching staff of eight was the standard. In the heat of a pennant race or in a World Series, however, regardless of the regular season rotation, the ace pitchers on the staff would take over with a short rest, sometimes starting on successive days. Often only two pitchers would carry the load. Remember the refrain "Give us Spahn and Sain and two days' rain"? Unusual, but reflective of Branch Rickey's dictum, "In baseball, subtraction is addition"—which is another way of saying, "Use your best players." That's how the game was played in those early days.

The 1920s and 1930s had a number of relief pitching specialists, but not as many as there are today. Among the best were Firpo Marberry, Wilcy Moore, Johnny Morrison, Johnny Murphy, Clint Brown, and Mace Brown. Except for Marberry, they were not the overpowering fastball pitchers in the style of Goose Gossage, Lee Smith, or Todd Worrell. They relied upon breaking balls, interspersed with an occasional strategic spitter. Morrison's overhand curveball (called a downer) was probably the best in baseball in those days. He was appropriately nicknamed "Jug-handle Johnny," which had nothing to do with his ears. Not every club had a reliever of that quality, but they would make up for that deficiency in a most effective way. In a critical situation, the last inning particularly, it was common practice to bring in the ace of the staff even though he may have pitched a full game the day before. Hitters had to contend with ninth-inning relievers such as Walter Johnson, Bob Grove, George Earnshaw, Rube Walberg, Lefty Gomez, Red Ruffing, Tommy Bridges, Mel Harder, Willis Hudlin, Carl Hubbell, Dazzy Vance, Dizzy Dean, Lon Warneke, Van Mungo, and Curt Davis.

Jimmie Reese tells of a game between the Yankees and the Philadelphia A's in 1930:

> It's the last of the ninth in Yankee Stadium. We're one run behind, the bases are loaded with nobody out. Our next three hitters are Ruth, Gehrig, and Lazzeri. Here comes Bob Grove in relief. He pitched the day before. He throws only *10* pitches and strikes out the side. Only Lazzeri was able to foul-tip a pitch. Nobody could have hit Grove that day.

Of course, not every ace of a pitching staff in the twenties and thirties could accomplish Bob Grove's feat against the Yankees. But with the game on the line, it was certain that one of the aces on the staff would be used in that spot. That was relief pitching at its best.

9

Fundamentals—What Are They Talking About?

In the fourth game of the 1987 World Series, Tom Lawless hit a home run, with runners on first and third, giving his St. Louis Cardinal team a 4–2 win over the Minnesota Twins. No player on the Cardinals could have hit a home run off Frank Viola, the ace of the Minnesota staff, and produced greater surprise than Lawless. It was his first homer since 1984 and only the second of his career.

Yet what was more mystifying was Lawless' reaction to his astonishing hit. He took a step or two and then remained stationary, as if transfixed, until the ball cleared the wall—barely. His explanation: "It was either a home run or a sacrifice fly out. It didn't make any difference if I ran or not."

Wrong.

There was another, more likely alternative. The ball could have caromed off the top of the wall. By not running, Lawless could have been held to a single on a ball that was a sure double and probably a triple. It would have meant a narrow 3–2 lead for the Cardinals and a huge psychological lift for Minnesota. Had the ball hit the wall and the Cardinals lost that game because of Lawless' failure to run and put himself into scoring position, Lawless could be wearing the horns of a goat instead of the laurels of a hero. By a margin of a few inches, he avoided a niche of ignominy in baseball that could have rivaled the base-running blunder by the unfortunate Fred Merkle in 1908.

Lawless violated the most fundamental precept in baseball: Hustle. Baseball managers rarely agree on any of baseball's so-called fundamentals. But they will agree 100 percent of the time that hustling is an absolute must, as basic to baseball as wheels to an automobile.

Another example. In the sixth game of that World Series, in Minnesota, Willie McGee was on first base when a fly ball was hit into short right center. Although the ball was landing safely, McGee ambled into second when he could have reached third without a throw. How was that possible? McGee is an excellent player with great speed; he plays hard and is recognized as a hustler, as is Lawless. There is no explanation for Lawless' lapse. McGee's lapse is something else. Here's what Hank Greenberg had to say about base running in an interview before his untimely death:

> Going from first to third on a base hit is not a matter of great speed as much as it is alertness. When on base, I knew where every outfielder was stationed. I knew something about their throwing abilities. I anticipated the bounce of the ball and the degree of difficulty the outfielder might have in handling it. Was he likely to wait for it to reach him—or even back up? This sounds complicated but it isn't. All it requires is a bit of alertness and anticipation.

McGee failed to be aware of "where every outfielder was stationed," as Greenberg counseled. That was a lapse in alertness, another fundamental.

When a manager talks about fundamentals, he is generally talking about three aspects of baseball: the hit and run; hitting a ground ball behind a runner on second base with no one out, so as to advance the runner to third; and for outfielders, to hit the cutoff man on throws to the plate or third base. The value of these three plays is debatable.

Branch Rickey, a recognized baseball authority, disdained the hit-and-run play, declaring that it "should be put on the shelf and forgotten." What's wrong with this tactic? Ralph Kiner, a Hall of Fame player, a disciple of Rickey, and perhaps Rickey's most tenacious combatant in salary disputes, made this observation:

> I don't entirely agree with Branch Rickey. He was looking at baseball as it was played 40, 50, and 60 years ago, when baseball was loaded with hitting talent. They didn't need the hit-and-run play. Ordinarily, you don't want to take the bat out of the hands of hitters. It was probably not a good play in Rickey's day, when there were lots of good hitters who could advance runners. The situation in baseball is different today. There are not that many good hitters. There are many weak, ground-ball hitters, and unless you start the runner with a hit-and-run, you invite double plays. So what might not have been fundamentally sound in the early days may be good strategy today.

Rickey's comment was made about 30 years ago. Today he would most likely agree with Kiner's view.

Hitting behind the runner is a favorite in the repertoire of almost every manager today. With a runner on second base and no one out, the idea is to hit a ground ball to the right side of the infield, with the object of advancing the runner from second base to third.

For a left-handed hitter this should be relatively easy. His natural swing is to the right side. The problem is with the right-handed hitters, who have to employ an unnatural batting swing to accomplish that objective. Al Lopez offers his opinion:

> That has never seemed to me to be good strategy, although it seems to be a standard procedure now. My feeling is that it takes something away from the hitter and that he often doesn't accomplish his objective. His natural swing might produce better results in the long run. It seems like a "give-up" play to me.

Kiner also has some reservations about that strategy. He asks: "If all that is wanted is to move the runner from second to third, wouldn't a bunt toward first base accomplish the same result and with less chance of failure?"

The "chance of failure" that Kiner refers to is due to the difficulty for a right-handed hitter in successfully delivering a ground ball to the second baseman. By taking a natural swing, the batter might get a base hit, even a long fly ball on which the runner could tag up and advance to third. Or he might even hit a slow ground ball to the infield, which is enough to advance the runner. The media and the fans may applaud the attempted hit-behind-the-runner maneuver by a right-handed hitter, but they get little support from the old-timers.

It was Branch Rickey's contention that the one incurable flaw in batting was overstriding, lunging at the pitch. He said: "I have never known a definite overstrider who became a regular in a major league lineup. I've discussed this many times with John McGraw and Mr. Mack, without disagreement. All great hitters are short striders."

Mr. Rickey should have discussed this with Lefty O'Doul, a great hitter in his day and an outstanding manager in the Pacific Coast League. He would have learned about one exception—Ferris Fain. Years ago, O'Doul explained to me his experiment with Fain:

> When I had Ferris Fain at San Francisco, he was the worst overstrider I had ever seen. He had so much baseball talent that I was determined to cure him of that batting fault. I couldn't see any reason why he should continue to hit .230. I got him to let me tie a rope to his front foot, around his ankle. I extended the other end of the rope through the batting cage and held the rope tight so that Fain's front foot couldn't move more than a few inches. At first he felt he would fall or get killed by a pitch. We kept up this routine until he got adjusted to *not* striding. Eventually we sold him to the majors where he became a good hitter—even leading the league in hitting one year.

I was intrigued with this story from the time O'Doul told it to me years ago. I spoke about it to Ferris Fain himself, who told me:

It's true, although the rope was attached through the belt loop in my uniform. Maybe at my ankle at first—but mostly it was tied to the loop. O'Doul broke me of that overstride. Hitting became easier and more enjoyable. I also learned something else about hitting from O'Doul that many of his other players also did. We used the O'Doul swing. We shortened up on the bat handle and sighted the pitch over the front elbow, as if we were looking through the gun sight of a rifle. He was one helluva guy and a great teacher.

A while back, an article by Bob Broeg appeared in the *Baseball Digest* under the title "Why So Many 'Lollipop' Arms among Outfielders." He asked, "Why is it that big league players don't throw as they used to, specially outfielders?"

Whitey Herzog answered: "They play a lazy game of catch before beginning a game. That's no way to build and strengthen a throwing arm."

Gene Mauch had another view in that same article: "It may be because football and basketball and other sports pay well, too, and baseball doesn't get so many great all-around players. But the truth is I don't see enough ball clubs exercise their outfielders with deep throws."

Today's emphasis on outfielders hitting the cutoff man when throwing to the plate brings into focus the quality of an outfielder's arm. Hank Greenberg made this observation:

A strong throwing arm was a prerequisite of every outfielder during the early days. Although a strong arm is a natural gift, even an ordinary throwing arm can be improved with practice. When I was in the minor leagues, we often would practice long hard throws from the outfield to home plate, even if some of us weren't outfielders. We developed our throwing arms. You couldn't become a regular outfielder on a major league club unless you could make a hard, one-bounce throw to the plate. Not many outfielders can do that today. So they have to hit the cutoff man for a relay. Or the cutoff has now become a decoy to trap the hitter, who might be attempting to take an extra base on the throw. A player has to be running with his head down to fall into that trap. He should know if there is a possibility of a play at the plate, or if the throw is likely to be cut off.

In addition to the fundamentals we've just examined, there are other basic aspects of play, that many fans are unfamiliar with. Looking for these—and detecting them—can made a fan's day or night at the ball park.

For example, why do outfielders and infielders move before a pitch is delivered? This maneuver, which has existed for as long as baseball has been played, is based upon the fact that an early movement by outfielders and infielders provides them with a quicker jump on a batted ball. Golfers will understand this. In golf, it's called the forward press. Simply put, the players are revving their engines, getting themselves into gear before the action starts. Oddly enough, in baseball this works effectively even though a ball may be hit in the direction opposite to the player's initial movement. Any movement in any direction is better than starting from a flat-footed position.

There are other subtleties in baseball that are more difficult to discern. For example, fans may be impressed with what appears to be a great catch by an outfielder. Yet the professional may see in that particular play an outfielder who was out of position in the first place or who got a slow jump on the ball, making a difficult catch out of what should have been a routine play. Joe DiMaggio spent his entire career making routine catches of fly balls that many other outfielders wouldn't have reached. That may be one reason why Bucky Harris stated that Joe DiMaggio was the greatest player he ever saw.

Stealing a base in baseball is an overt act that is appreciated and applauded by even the most puritanical of fans. Yet this bit of thievery is not the same class as stealing a catcher's signs.

A catcher's signs are generally stolen by the coaches, who inch their way out of the coach's box to get a sidelong, unobtrusive peek at the catcher's signals. These signals are easy to decode inasmuch as most clubs use the same set of signs. The catcher's signs indicate the type of pitch to be made, which should be valuable information to the hitter. Yet many hitters do not want such information. It upsets their concentration. It creates a small but disturbing doubt in their minds: "What if the information is wrong? I may be leaning in, looking for a curve, and instead it's a fastball at my head, and I can't duck the pitch in time."

The genius in sign stealing is such that its victims are rarely aware of it. It is among the rarest and most prized of all baseball strategies, and when properly executed, it produces maximum rewards, such as winning ball games. It can even lead to a pennant. That happened in 1940, when Detroit edged Cleveland by a margin of one game. It was the year Hank Greenberg legitimately "stole" the pennant for Detroit.

Hitters who have confidence in stolen signs thrive on that intelligence with remarkable results. Hank Greenberg was that type of hitter. He had two of the best sign stealers in baseball as coaches during his career—Del Baker and Charlie Dressen. I asked Greenberg which of those two was the more effective sign stealer.

> They were both good. The difference was that Baker was quiet about it, and Dressen would talk and boast. I loved to get the signs and so did Rudy York. If I definitely knew what was coming up, I could hit anybody. I never considered myself a "guess" hitter. I'd prefer to think that I was an intelligent hitter. Yet the greatest results I ever had from knowing the signs didn't originate from the coaches. It occurred in an unusual way.
>
> In the last part of the 1940 season, Tommy Bridges showed up in the dugout before a game, carrying a rifle with a high-powered telescopic lens. He was a hunter and had just purchased the rifle to take home with him after the season. Some of us looked through the lens and were astonished how close the most distant objects appeared. Someone suggested that we equip one of our bullpen pitchers with

high-powered binoculars to zero in on the catcher's signs. Then, by a hand signal, the catcher's sign could be relayed directly to the batter. The distance between us was barely more than a hundred yards, so we could easily spot the sign from the bullpen or from the outfield fence. In that month of September 1940, the year we won the pennant, I had the greatest hitting stretch in my career. From September 4th to September 26, 1940, in 22 games, I hit .410, with 34 hits in 82 at-bats. I had 15 homers, scored 32 runs, and batted in 38.

During a part of that month we were playing the Yankees, and Joe McCarthy was getting suspicious. It seemed as if every ball I hit was a "frozen rope." Our guy with the binoculars had to move into the outfield stands. Of course, he'd be in street clothes, a pitcher who wasn't working that day. He blended in with the fans, but we could still spot him and get the signs. This wasn't an entirely new tactic. Many clubs, from time to time, were doing the same thing by focusing their binoculars through openings in the outfield scoreboards. I never had a more enjoyable month than September 1940.

Greenberg's achievements in September of 1940 may very well have been the most productive 22-game batting spree in baseball's history. It won a pennant for Detroit.

Perhaps no fundamental in baseball is more simple and bungled more often than the sacrifice bunt. The execution of this bunt, or the lack of execution, often determines the outcome of a game. The weaker the hitter, the more critical it is for him to be able to lay down a bunt. In the National League, which does not operate with a designated hitter, it is imperative for the pitchers to master the technique of bunting. Yet failure is a common result. Sacrifice bunting does not require hitting ability or any special talent. There is no justification for major league players, and particularly pitchers, not knowing how to execute this simple yet important procedure.

In a discussion with Jigger Statz, he expressed his surprise at the ineffective bunting by current-day major league players:

There are two basic rules in bunting. One, the bat must make contact with the ball in *fair* territory. I see players trying to bunt with their bats behind the plate. That is foul territory and the balls will roll foul. The second basic is to hold the bat level to the ground. There are other refinements—such as, don't jab at the ball, let the ball hit the bat. But the major requirements are to keep the bat in fair territory and level. I see players desperately trying to bunt even with two strikes—a risk that we rarely needed to take in the old days.

Johnnie Kerr talked about bunting:

Bunting was something that we learned in the minor leagues and which should never have to be taught in the majors. Bunting is no big deal. You give yourself up. That means, turn around, face the pitcher, extend your arms, and "catch" the ball on your bat —sort of bring your bat back as if it's a glove and not a bat. It's often a crucial play, and every major leaguer should be able to accomplish it.

Yet this fundamental tactic is often so poorly executed that it's no longer shocking to see players bunting with two strikes, which often results in a foul ball and an automatic out. Where to bunt may require some judgment, but how to bunt is the simplest of all batting techniques. It was rare for a player in the 1920s and 1930s to be bunting with a two-strike count.

After Billy Martin returned for the fourth time to the New York Yankees in 1986, succeeding Yogi Berra, he criticized the general manager of the Yankees for the team's failure to execute fundamentals. The fundamentals that he referred to were the old familiar clichés —rundowns, cutoffs, and hit-and-run plays. "A lot of things have to be corrected here," he fumed, "but these things should have been done in spring training. . . . What do they do in spring training?"

Billy Martin knows the answer to that question. He knows that spring training is not the place for learning the fundamentals of baseball. That may seem to be the time and place for it, but it doesn't happen, although all managers talk about it. Spring training camps today are cluttered with an excessive number of players—minor leaguers, free agents, as well as the regular members of the club. There are too many players in the camps to devote time to the intensive practice of fundamentals, which should have been learned in the minor leagues under game conditions. Spring training primarily affords the young prospects a chance to get a taste of the major league environment, while giving the manager a chance to observe and appraise any new, potentially major-league talent. But it is not conducive for developing baseball's fundamental techniques.

In 1985, the St. Louis Cardinals and the Kansas City Royals battled in a dramatic seven-game World Series. In the fifth and sixth games, the Cardinal catchers committed devastating errors in fundamentals that lost the World Series for the Cardinals. Although those errors were in full view of millions of fans and hundreds of media observers, no one recognized those lapses; no one spoke about them, nor were they referred to in print. Undoubtedly Whitey Herzog, manager of the Cardinals, and the players saw them. Here is what happened.

At critical junctures in the Series, each of the Cardinal catchers, Nieto and Porter, had an easy tag play at the plate on Jim Sundberg of the Royals. In both instances, they failed to execute the tags. Nieto's lapse gave the Royals three leading runs in the fifth game; Porter gave them the winning run in the sixth game. Had the Cardinals won either game, they would have won the World Series.

With some perplexity, *The Sporting News Annual Guide* summed up the fifth game with the observation that "Cedeno's throw beat Sundberg by five feet," and yet Sundberg was called safe. With equal puzzlement, the guide referred to the sixth game, stating: "Sundberg slid around Porter's tag, although Van Slyke's throw appeared in plenty of time for Porter to make the tag." How could Sundberg have been safe if the throws arrived in ample time for the catchers to make the tags? Here's why.

In baseball, it's a de facto rule that umpires favor the runner if an infielder or a catcher makes a reach-back tag, as Nieto and Porter did. Each of these catchers unnecessarily abandoned his position at the plate, moved up the line to take the throw, then turned back to the plate to make the tag. Those are reach-back tags—basic errors in the fundamentals of play. Umpires assume that a runner's hand or leg will have reached the plate or bag before the tag is applied to the some other part of the runner's anatomy. Were the tags made on Sundberg before his hand touched the plate? Probably so. But it made no difference. Umpires do not call runners out on reach-back tags. Is it a coincidence that Nieto and Porter were not with the Cardinals the following year? Avoiding reach-back tags is especially important for infielders.

Jimmie Reese had this to say on the subject:

> Umpires will never give an infielder the decision if he *reaches back* to make a tag. It's possible that the tag was made in time, but the umpires are automatic on reach-back tags. I suppose they feel that a player's foot or hand reaches the bag before the tag is made on the runner.

Johnnie Kerr explained:

> Unless there is no alternative because the throw is off-line, an infielder must never take a throw in *front* of the bag. You can stay behind the bag or straddle it—but you won't get the call if you take a throw in front of the bag and then reach back to tag the runner. Actually, you let the runner tag himself out by his sliding into the glove. You have to be careful because some runners will try to kick the ball out of the glove. This doesn't happen too often today, since most runners today dive into a bag. Tagging a player's hand gives you a small target, but there is no deception in this slide. Ballplayers used to slide two or three different ways. But regardless of the type of slide, the infielder, wherever possible, should never take throws in front of the bag and then reach back to make a tag.

Perhaps no player influenced the artistry of sliding into bases, more than Ty Cobb. He had no greater admirer than Ossie Bluege, who described Cobb's techniques:

> The headfirst slide that is common today was rarely used in the twenties and thirties. Ty Cobb influenced running and sliding styles, just as Babe Ruth influenced hitting. Many runners would make a wide sweep around first base on the way to second. Not Cobb. He would go straight for the bag, hit it with his left foot, tilt his body toward second, and never break stride. If a tag play was imminent, Cobb would employ one of several sliding methods. He could sense the direction of the throw by the position of the infielder. He would then *fake* a slide as if he was going directly at the infielder, but at the last moment he would throw his body in the opposite direction, away from the infielder and the bag. He would overslide the bag, then reach for a corner of it with his hand. He gave the infielder the smallest possible target. He could make this slide going to his left or to his right. Of course, if those deceptive moves weren't needed, he'd come directly at the bag, straight and hard. It was no picnic trying to tag Ty Cobb.

Ozzie Smith is probably the best tagger of all infielders in baseball. He waits on a throw until the runner is virtually on top of him, and gets the runner to tag himself out. Smith has the agility to avoid getting knocked off his feet, and he tags base runners from every conceivable angle. By observing how he positions himself on a potential tag play, fans will be able to appreciate a special part of the artistry in baseball.

Another feature of Ozzie Smith's talent is the quick, accurate, chest-high throw that he makes to his second baseman on potential double plays. He can make any second baseman look good. A second baseman who has to reach, high or low, for inaccurate or late throws by his shortstop often finds himself on the ground before the play is over. He becomes an easy target for a sliding runner. This is another of the important things that the professionals see and admire in Ozzie Smith—he protects his second basemen.

Shortstops are judged on their ability to go into the "hole," the area between short and third, to retrieve a ground ball and successfully make the long throw to first. That is probably as good a test as any in gauging the talent of a shortstop. Ozzie Smith can make plays from the hole that no other shortstop has been able to accomplish—or is supposed to accomplish. Where the average shortstop would be happy just to knock the ball down, Ozzie Smith can dive into the hole for it, jump to his feet, and make the throw to first—in one apparently unbroken motion. It's an almost unbelievable play, and he does it repeatedly.

If Whitey Herzog says that Smith saves the Cardinals "a hundred runs a year" with his defense, that does not seem like an exaggeration. Smith's glove work wins ball games that statistics cannot calculate.

Has any fan ever had the feeling that an infielder may have taken his foot off a base prematurely? Don't doubt your judgment. On double plays, the infielders *do* come off the bag a split second before the ball reaches them. But the umpire's call never varies. A runner is always "out" as long as the ball beats him to the bag, even though the infielder's foot may be off the bag. Infielders cannot make it too obvious. But this "cheating" by an infielder—taking his foot off the bag a fraction of a second before the ball arrives, to avoid a sliding runner—is accepted by the teams and the umpires.

The mounting increase in stolen bases and its various causes have been much discussed. One of the contributing factors, however, has gone pretty much unnoticed: first basemen with the bad habit of extending their gloved hands toward the pitcher with a runner on first base. Reaching for a ball and turning to make a tag loses a fraction of a second, which is often the difference between "out" and "safe."

Hank Greenberg said:

I don't recall any first baseman, years ago, who stretched his arm toward the pitcher while holding a runner on first. I don't know the purpose of this style. Are they trying to give the pitcher a target to throw to? If so, that's the wrong target. It should be low and to the bag, where the tag can be made.

Ossie Bluege made this comment:

It's not necessary to throw to first base unless you've got a runner leaning and a first baseman who can apply a quick tag. Otherwise, just hold the ball. Watch the runner, and sooner or later he'll relax or give himself away—so that the pitcher can throw to the plate before the runner gets a big jump. There was a pitcher in the 1920s, Sad Sam Jones, who never threw to first base. Everyone knew it, yet you couldn't steal on him. The best "taggers" among the first baseman in those days were Joe Kuhel and Joe Judge. Kuhel was especially quick, although I considered Judge the best defensive first baseman of them all. Even better than Sisler, who was no slouch around the bag.

In baseball's early years, the major leaguers executed some plays with a dispatch not seen in baseball today. One example is the "rundown" between third and home. Regardless of the end result, this play is not handled in the major leagues today as it was in the 1920s and 1930s.

Every manager agrees that the rundown play requires only one throw to retire a trapped runner and that the batter should never be permitted to take an extra base. What we often see is confusion, throws going back and forth, with the trapped runner often retired at the wrong base. What should be a routine play too often ends with the batter taking an extra base. Thus, the batter ends up in scoring position, which was exactly what the trapped runner was trying to accomplish in the first place. The old-timers had no problem with this play.

Ossie Bluege explained the proper technique:

We were never concerned about the trapped runner. We knew we were going to get him. What we wanted was the batter as he rounded first base. We were looking for two outs, not one. I recall this play against two of the best base runners that ever played the game, Eddie Collins and Ty Cobb, when they were with the Philadelphia Athletics in 1927. Collins was on third base in the ninth inning, one run behind and one out. Cobb was at the plate, and he hit the ball to me at third. As Collins broke for home, I threw the ball to our catcher, Muddy Ruel. Now Collins is trapped between home and third. Collins wants to stall—to give Cobb a chance to get to second, to get into scoring position. As soon as I threw to the plate, I ran up alongside of Collins, on the infield side of the diamond. The shortstop covered third base for me. At that instant Ruel snapped the ball to me, I tagged Collins, then threw to second base—and now we got Cobb trapped and retired him for a double play. I remember that game particularly, because Cobb ran toward Collins and shouted at him, "How long have you been playing the game?" That was really funny. The key to this play is the catcher. He must not fake a throw. He must make his snap throw when the third baseman is alongside of the trapped runner. You don't see that play these days. All it takes is a little practice.

An obvious change over the years has been the introduction of the oversized gloves used today by infielders and outfielders. These are basketlike traps in comparison to the gloves of the twenties and thirties. How much of an advantage are the large gloves? Jimmie Reese expressed this view:

> The large gloves are a major advantage to outfielders but less so to the infielders. It extends the reach of outfielders and infielders. However, it often poses a problem for infielders because they can't quickly dislodge the ball from the glove. The loss of a split second because a ball is stuck in an infielder's glove is often the difference in completing the double play. That problem rarely occurred with the smaller gloves.

Babe Herman explained the value of the larger gloves in the outfield:

> Today there are more diving catches in the outfield in one month than I saw in my entire career. The big gloves that the outfielders now use make it possible for them to make diving catches, or at least knock

down the ball. The small gloves we used were not likely to hold the ball if we dove for it. If we missed, we would be giving up a double or a triple. It would have been too risky for us.

Willie Kamm had some reservations about the large gloves and diving for balls by infielders:

> The larger gloves may have something to do with it, yet I can't under-stand all this diving on ground balls. That's something we seldom did. When you dive for a ball, the chances are that you will not come up with it cleanly. It can easily roll away a few feet, far enough to lose a play at first, for example. If you stay on your feet and fumble a ball, it's generally in front of you, where you can still make the play. I don't think a third baseman can get to a ball more quickly by diving after it than by staying upright and taking a quick step or two.

The fundamentals in baseball are not only physical techni-ques. Psychological tactics are also an elementary part of the game and were taught even in the minor leagues.

I recall playing for "Dutch" Zwilling in St. Joseph, Missouri, in the Western League. Tactics were his forte. He pounded at us with this concept:

> Don't look at their batting or fielding practices. Don't watch their pitchers warming up. Be disdainful of them, as if they have nothing to interest you. Adopt the attitude that you are superior to them from the moment you walk on the ball field and you'll be playing that way.

Not bad advice. This psychological ploy is more effective than one might think. Remember the stories about the 1927 World Series between Pittsburgh and the New York Yankees, which the Yankees won in four straight games. The press insisted that the Pirates were intimidated by watching Babe Ruth, Lou Gehrig, and company pound ball after ball out of the park in batting practice.

A few exceptions are justified. "Everyone stopped to watch Babe Ruth take his swings in batting practice," said Hank Green-berg. "He was something special."

Ted Williams received similar attention, even when he was 18 years old on the 1937 San Diego club. I know, because I was on that club then. No one had ever seen a swing like Williams'. As with Babe Ruth, it was an experience for the players of both teams to watch Williams swing a bat. Yet despite his great natural swing, Williams could not have become the remarkable hitter that he was without his countless hours of batting practice. It is doubtful that any player in the game devoted more time than Williams to analyzing, refining, and perfecting the techniques of hitting. Williams became so disciplined at the plate that it was a rarity for him to swing at a pitch that was out of the strike zone. No player ever claimed, as Williams did, that a pitched ball seemed to "stop" for him, that he could see the bat make contact with the ball.

Babe Ruth's hitting approach was in reverse of Williams. Jimmie Reese, a roommate of Babe Ruth, said:

> It is doubtful if Ruth ever gave a thought to tinkering with his batting stroke or concerning himself with the strike zone. He was, in a sense, an undisciplined hitter relying entirely upon his natural talent and instincts. He had absolute confidence in his ability to hit any pitcher.

For example, Bob Grove was regarded as the best pitcher in the game during most of Babe Ruth's career. No one matched Grove's fast ball, his competitiveness, and his success. Yet Jimmie Reese recalls: "When Grove was due to pitch against us, the Babe would clap his hands and chortle, 'Lookie, lookie! Look who we got today. I'm going to get me a couple of big ones!'"

Two great hitters, Williams and Ruth, with diametrically opposite approaches to hitting, yet equally effective. Is it any wonder that the art of hitting is so baffling?

10

How Johnny Bench Ruined the Art of Catching

After Tom Seaver joined the Cincinnati team, following a long career with the New York Mets, he was asked about his adjustment to the change in catchers. With the Mets he pitched to Jerry Grote. In Cincinnati he was pitching to the highest-rated catcher in baseball, Johnny Bench. Seaver made a simple response without elaboration. The best catcher for him was Grote.

Seaver's comment made little impact on the media, although it was a significant statement. It touched upon the change in catching styles, from the two-handed method used by Grote to the one-handed style initiated and popularized by Johnny Bench.

This change in catching techniques has had far-reaching effects in baseball. If one item of play had to be selected to exemplify the difference between the style of the game in the 1920s and 1930s and the style of the game today, no better example exists than the radical change to the one-handed method of catching.

Let there be no misunderstanding. Johnny Bench was one of the best talents ever to play the game. He is a bona fide Hall of Fame candidate. His hitting and throwing ability ranks him among the best catchers in history. Yet his unsound style of one-handed catching set a harmful example for other catchers in baseball who do not measure up to his ability. Over the years, the result has been an excessive number of wild pitches and the loss to pitchers of an untold number of strikes.

In an article in *Sports Illustrated*, Bench explained his motivation for one-handed catching:

> I had the ability to change the game with the one-handed glove. I could stand away from a sliding runner and avoid a collision by making a sweeping tag. You just have to go "*Olé*," like making a tag at second. Catchers never had the time to do that when they had to use two hands with the round glove. You got to keep the glove moving to make the sweep tag; don't just put the glove in front of the runner's foot. It's like catching an egg and you got to give with it.

In the same article, the New York Mets broadcaster Tim McCarver, a former catcher, commented:

> Bench was the best one-handed catcher ever. . . . Birdie Tebbetts and others said to catch with two hands. When you catch one-handed, you can snap the ball to your throwing hand, whereas the movement is too bulky with two hands. . . . The other thing John popularized was the hinged glove, as opposed to the old ones with the little pocket in the middle. If you caught everything in the pocket, it would sting your hand, so you'd try to catch it in the webbing. If the ball sailed, you'd miss it. The new gloves are designed for catching the ball in the pocket without pain. . . . It's like a first baseman's glove. Now, if the ball sails, you catch it in the webbing.

These two well-known and respected catchers miss the point. Their concern for one-handed catching and its specially designed glove is centered on the benefits that accrue only to catchers. Not one word of recognition or consideration is given to the effects that this style of catching may have on the pitchers and on their teams.

One apparent reason for the one-handed style is to reduce the likelihood of a catcher breaking a finger, which could put him out of commission for two or three weeks. This is a valid consideration. Two-handed catching did expose a catcher's bare hand to foul tips and possible broken fingers. Such accidents were often the result of improper technique or carelessness and not typical of the good receivers. Bob Lemon, a Hall of Fame pitcher, said: "My catcher was Jim Hegan, one of the best in the business. In the years that he caught, I recall his breaking a finger only once, and that didn't keep him out of the lineup for more than a week or so."

An item in *The Sporting News* on the new mitt and the one-handed style of catching noted the opinion of Del Crandall, who is widely rated as an authority on the subject: "He believes that the new [catchers] gloves and Johnny Bench's one-handed technique have set back the art of receiving." Crandall is quoted:

> The new [glove] is like a first baseman's glove. I call it a picker's mitt. It tempts the catcher to snatch at the ball instead of moving into it. . . . I had only one broken finger [in 16 seasons] and that was in my last year. You see catchers with one hand behind the back. They may not realize it, but it has taken them back defensively. It causes all kinds of bad habits.

Sparky Anderson also expressed some doubts about the one-handed style:

> One-handed catching, particularly with palms down, is not the best way to receive a pitch. Many strikes are lost that way. It also results in more wild pitches. However, if it prevents a broken finger, I suppose that is a substantial offset.

The most significant disadvantage of one-handed catching is its tendency to reduce the strike zone. The basic theory in catching is to make every pitch look better than it really is. This requires almost imperceptible movements by the catcher. Low pitches must be guided upward into the strike zone, and high pitches downward. Above all, no radical movements of the glove. The more easily a catcher receives a pitch and the more subtle his movements, the more likely he will get the close calls. There is no greater advantage to a pitcher and to his club than to have a catcher convert a potential "ball" into a "strike." Conversely, there is no greater damage than to lose actual strikes by moving the glove out of the strike zone. The plate umpire, no matter how competent he may be, is not likely to call a strike on a close pitch that is propelled out of the strike zone by the catcher. There is, of course, no way of measuring the number of strikes that have been lost to pitchers because of the one-handed catching style. The loss of even a few, however, can often turn a win to a loss for a pitcher.

Many pitchers are effective *only* by pitching "low," around the knees. Bob Lemon was that kind of pitcher, and he expressed these views:

> I was strictly a low-ball pitcher but Hegan had the knack of smoothly bringing these pitches up into the strike zone, with two hands, and palms up. Most catchers with a one-handed style can't do that on low pitches. Their palms are down, making the pitch look bad. Umpires are human. If they see a catcher grabbing a pitch and pushing it out of the strike zone, their instincts are to call the pitch a ball.

Many catchers today have become what Wes Westrum calls "snatchers." They reach for the ball, "snatching" it, instead of "receiving" the pitch, in effect letting it settle into the glove. The process of reaching and snatching involves excessive hand action, invariably palms down on low pitches, making such pitches look worse than they really are.

Al Lopez made these observations during my discussions with him:

> There was no one-handed catching when I played or managed. Major league catchers caught to the center of their bodies. This had to be done with two hands, and as effortlessly as possible, to convince the umpire that the pitch was easy to handle and in the strike zone. This required a minimum of hand action, no grabbing or "boxing" a ball. I don't understand all the jumping around behind the plate that goes

on today. The pitchers have a hard enough time throwing strikes without the distraction of a "jumping jack" catcher. It's like throwing to a moving target. Catchers give away the location of the pitch by moving from one side to another. I know I had to be careful with some hitters, such as Billy Herman, Chuck Klein, and Lefty O'Doul. They would take a sly peek at me to see where I was located. If an outside pitch is required, a slight gesture such as leaning the shoulder is enough to get the message across to the pitcher. I see catchers station themselves outside of the strike zone, which the umpire easily recognizes, and so he will not call a strike.

Bibb Falk who coached the University of Texas team for 25 years after a successful professional career, had this to say:

> The problem with catching today is the glove. It's nothing more than an oversized first baseman's glove. That makes it conducive to one-handed catching, and to snatching the ball in the manner of a first baseman and often making good pitches look bad. These new gloves don't make the popping sound like the mitts the old-timers used. Pitchers liked to hear that loud pop.

Johnny Bench stresses that the new glove makes tagging easier. He refers to his one-handed *"olé"* tag at the plate. That is indeed a spectacular play, one that only Johnny Bench has been able to make. For all catchers, the normal play is for a catcher to position himself between the runner and the plate and apply the tag—not necessarily with the ball, but preferably with the back of the glove or through body contact with the runner. It is risky for a catcher or an infielder to expose his glove and the ball to the foot of a sliding runner. The hard-sliding runners of the 1920s and 1930s—such as Jo-Jo White with the Detroit Tigers, Ben Chapman with the Yankees and the Senators, or Ty Cobb—often used their "free" leg to kick balls out of players' gloves. A superstar such as Bench might have been able to make one-handed tags successfully, but for everyone else it is an unnecessary gamble.

McCarver makes the point that the one-handed catching style

permits a faster release of throws on potential stolen bases. No old-time catchers will agree with that opinion. One-handed reception of a baseball puts a catcher in an unbalanced throwing position. The catching style in the twenties and thirties was to "come out throwing," simultaneously with the base runner's start for second base. No one did it any better than Gabby Hartnett. He possessed a rifle arm, as great an arm as any catcher ever had. When he finished his throw to second base, he would often end up *in front of* the plate. He came out throwing, with a vengeance.

Al Lopez offered this additional observation:

Catchers today often receive the pitch flat-footed, or even on their heels. No one can get anything on a throw from that position. Visualize an outfielder and you'll get the idea. If he catches a ball leaning backward, he has to reposition himself to make the throw. If he is moving forward, he not only gets rid of the ball faster but he has more power on the throw. The same with catchers. They don't have to be snug up against the hitter. It's better for a catcher to be a half step further back so he can lean forward on his toes and move into the pitch. When I saw a runner breaking for second, I would start my forward motion *before* the pitcher released the ball. Obviously you can't interfere with the batter, but that rarely happened because I'd be moving away from the hitter at the time I was throwing. I don't see many good throwing catchers today. In the old days you couldn't become a regular major league catcher unless you could throw. I don't see what the new-style glove or the old glove has to do with proper throwing techniques. Of course, you can't be grabbing a pitch one-handed and out of position and expect to throw out a good base runner.

Is the new type of glove with its hinged webbing easier on a catcher's hand? Possibly—but no catcher in the twenties and thirties, or in any years prior to the introduction of the Johnny Bench glove, has ever expressed any concern over a ball "stinging" his hand, as Tim McCarver suggests. Nor did catchers deliberately "try to catch [pitches] in the webbing" to protect their hands, as he claims. Catchers never thought about such things.

No old-timer can recall any problems with the two-handed catching style or with the so-called "bulky" gloves and the presumed "little pocket in the middle." Most catchers used a sponge or a flat piece of rubber to absorb any shock. Catchers today wear a separate glove, perhaps a batting glove, inside their mitts. Yet none of these accoutrements are as important as "receiving" or "giving" with the pitch to lessen the impact of the ball. That was the catching style of the twenties and thirties.

The current one-handed method, which invites reaching and the "snatching" of pitches, can be a painful experience, which is perhaps alleviated by the hinged webbing that McCarver talks about. But that type of "pain" is a minor factor in catching, and it's surprising that McCarver would make a point of it.

It is a catcher's responsibility to prevent wild pitches that permit runners to advance a base and often score what should have been a preventable run. The two-handed catchers shifted on errant pitches, using their bodies and their bigger gloves to block a potential wild pitch. Many one-handed catchers try to accomplish the same result by reaching for the ball, relying more upon their gloves than their bodies. It sometimes happens that a batter with two strikes will swing and strike out on a pitch in the dirt. This third strike often eludes the catcher, permitting batters to reach first base safely.

There is, however, one statistic that provides an indication of the damage produced by one-handed catching. This applies to the mounting number of wild pitches that have been occurring since 1968, when the one-handed style was developed by Johnny Bench.

As one-handed catching became the vogue, wild pitches increased. Understandably, not all catchers adopted this new mode of catching at the outset. The conversion was gradual. Today all catchers employ the Bench technique. The table below demonstrates the results.

WILD PITCHES—COMBINED LEAGUES
Adjusted to 16 teams, 154-game schedule

	Combined League Yearly Average	Per Team Average
1948-67	552	35
1968-87†	703	44

† 1981 strike year excluded.

For the years 1968 through 1987, when one-handed catching became the fashion, the average number of wild pitches per year is more than 25 percent greater than the average for the preceding 20 years, 1948 through 1967. The precise cost of this excess cannot be calculated. Yet it is obviously costly to give base runners an extra base or run because of ineffective attempts to block pitches with one hand.

In the 20-year comparisons, were pitching styles different that could have had a bearing on wild pitches? There is no way to make such a determination. There were changes in pitching styles, but with offsets of one type or another. The slider is a prominent and dominating pitch today, more so than in the twenties and thirties. It is a fastball with a twist that veers away from a hitter. It may be a difficult pitch for the hitter but should pose no problem for the catcher. He knows what pitch is on the way and should be ready to shift in the direction of the pitch. There is no reason why the slider should be a factor in the excessive number of wild pitches. Knuckleballs are the toughest pitches to catch and the most likely to create problems for a catcher. There is, however, nothing new about knuckleball pitching. It has been in use for at least 75 years.

Some wild pitches have no effect on the outcome of a game. Many others can turn a game around. Part of the damage is the adverse psychological effect it has on the pitchers. Pitchers are more effective if they can pitch with full confidence in their catchers. They need that inner assurance that they can cut loose with their pitches without worrying about potentially wild pitches.

The aesthetics of these two catching styles is not at issue. What is involved is the necessity of converting balls into strikes and preventing wild pitches that give away unnecessary runs. At stake is the outcome of a game.

11 The Balk Rule— The Umpires' True Love

No rule in baseball is more bewildering in the game today than the balk rule. What makes this rule so unusual is that no one really understands it. It is a mystery to the managers, players, and fans alike. Its perplexity extends even to the umpires. Everyone understands the penalty but not the infraction. Ron Luciano, a long-time major league umpire, now retired, made this acknowledgment in an interview in *The Sporting News:* "I never called a balk in my life. I didn't understand the rule and I still don't. Every time Gene Mauch tried to explain it to me, it got more confusing, so I didn't bother with it."

The basic intent of the balk rule is to prohibit a pitcher from deceiving a runner on first base by pretending to throw to first or to the plate but doing the opposite. That is clearly a violation—a balk. Balks may result from other infractions. But the most common balks are those that occur when a pitcher is trying to hold a runner on first base. It wasn't always so.

From baseball's earliest years up to 1974, pitchers operated in a wide gray area of the rule known as the "half-balk." Although no such official designation or modification of the balk rule has ever existed, the half-balk was accepted on the same basis as certain other de facto practices that exist in the game today. For example, there's the automatic "safe" call on a reach-back tag, and there's the "out" decision at second base even though the infielder's foot may be off the bag when the ball arrives. There are rarely any arguments on those plays.

Under the half-balk precept, pitchers developed a variety of deceptive head movements, leg pivots, and body gestures that were accepted as legitimate pitching techniques. Left-handers, especially, gave runners no easy clue whether a pitch would be thrown to the plate or to first base. Pitchers were allowed reasonable latitude to contain potential base stealers, holding them closer to the bag and preventing running starts.

In the twenties and thirties, the stolen base was a risk and an achievement. It was not attempted except in special situations where one run was a factor. Base stealing was not for everybody. Jigger Statz, one of baseball's best base runners, commented on the strategies of base stealing during those years when he played for the New York Giants under John McGraw, and subsequently with the Chicago Cubs, when Bill Killefer was manager:

> In those days, runners did not run on their own initiative. You waited for a sign from the coach or from the bench. It was a risky business to try to steal on some pitchers. Some left-handed pitchers could pick you off if you were just leaning to second base, even though you were only a step or two off the bag. It was a real challenge to steal a base in those days and attempted only under special circumstances.

The half-balk kept runners virtually tied to the bag. It was dangerous to venture more than a step or two off first base. Al Lopez describes an experience in 1930, when he was breaking into the major leagues: "We're in the Polo Grounds playing the New York Giants. They got Clarence Mitchell, an old time left-hand spitballer, pitching for them. He picks me off twice in one game. And I wasn't even thinking of running."

Babe Herman described the moves of some pitchers:

> Of the pitchers I saw, Roy Joiner had the best move. He learned it from Dutch Reuther, who was real good. But Joiner was unusually deceptive. He would make a couple of decoy throws to first base. When he wanted to pick you off, he made an entirely different throw, some

thing the runner hadn't seen before. He did a slight shuffle with his feet, which looked like he was pitching to the plate but the ball would be on the way to first. Among the right-handers, "Wiz" Kremer had a great move that couldn't be detected. So did Dolf Luque and "Rip" Sewell. What these pitchers had in common was their quick release to the plate. Today everything those pitchers did would be called balks.

The most effective move to first base in my experience was that of Herman "Old Folks" Pillette, my teammate on the 1937 San Diego Padres. He had a career that covered 25 years, mostly in the Coast League. Everyone liked him, including the umpires, who overlooked his tendency to commit the most outrageous balks. Occasionally, in a critical part of a game, he would even scratch up a pile of loose dirt with his spikes and cover the pitching rubber. Pretty soon he'd be pitching inches in front of the concealed rubber. That's a balk in anybody's league. To the hitters, it must have looked as if Pillette was about to step on them.

I recall one game particularly. We were playing Portland and I was catching Pillette. In those days, only two umpires worked our games. Behind the plate was Sam Crawford. It was hard to imagine that this was the same great Sam Crawford whose reputation as a player during the early years of baseball was that of a tough, battling competitor. As an umpire, Sam was a pussy cat. He may not have been the most talented umpire, but he was certainly the most gentle, the kindest person ever to wear an umpire's uniform. Confrontations saddened him. I could never criticize a decision of Sam's without subsequent feelings of remorse and guilt.

Pillette had a long, lazy delivery that would make present-day base runners drool. But you couldn't run on him. As is often the case in baseball, senior-citizen players get preferential treatment from the umpires. With Pillette it took the form of tolerance for his overt balk moves and granting him a larger strike zone, which was not unreasonable considering his advanced age and benign disposition.

In that game with Portland, we were in the ninth inning and one run ahead. A Portland runner, the potential tying run, reached first base. Pillette's first pitch to the next hitter never got there. It seemed that Herm changed his mind while in the act of delivering the pitch to the plate. He short-circuited and changed directions. Whoosh! The ball was now on the way to first base where the unsuspecting runner was neatly picked off base. It was a virtuoso balk. On the Richter scale of balks, an absolute 10.

Out comes Bill Sweeney, the Portland manager, whose disposition ran the gamut from raging fury to physical violence. He was screaming at Sam Crawford: "Sam! Sam! Did you see that? That is the goddamnedest balk I've ever seen." Me, too. I never saw a balk like that one. Herman came ambling to the plate, trying to pacify Sweeney. As I recall, the conversation went like this:

PILLETTE: Take it easy, Bill. You know I always pitch like that. What are you trying to do? Take the bread out of my mouth?

CRAWFORD: That's right, Bill. He's always pitched that way.

SWEENEY: Bullshit! Herm, you know I never complain when you pitch a foot in front of the rubber. But that was a goddamned balk. The guys on my bench are hollering.

PILLETTE: They're a bunch of crybabies. And I never take 12 inches. Maybe 6—but not 12.

CRAWFORD: That's true. Herm, can you tone it down a bit?

PILLETTE: I'll try, Sam. Sorry to cause you any trouble.

SWEENEY: Yeah. I hope I haven't been too rough on you, Sam.

CRAWFORD: That's OK. Can we get on with the game?

I stood by listening to this without saying a word, not believing what I was hearing. These three guys were actually apologizing to each other!

Despite the half-balk moves in the earlier years, some base runners countered with unusual techniques. Ben Chapman, for example. I was on the Washington club in 1936 when Chapman was traded to the Senators by the New York Yankees for Jake Powell. Chapman was not a particularly friendly fellow, but that made no difference. He could play. He was an exceptional base runner and one of the hardest sliders in the league. It was dangerous to try to pick him off first base. His technique was simple, direct, and dramatically effective. He would time a pitcher's throw to first so that he and the ball would arrive at the same time, permitting him to slide into the first baseman and flip him. He'd take the first baseman out of the play. With no one to catch the toss, the ball would go bouncing down the line, with Chapman ending up at second or third. Sometimes he'd retreat directly into the path of the ball. It would hit him on the back and bounce out of reach, and again he'd end up with an extra base. Now there was a player who could unnerve two players at a time—the pitcher and the first baseman. No headfirst slides into the base for Chapman. The first baseman was his target, not the bag.

Where balks were once a rarity, they became a major factor in 1974, resulting in some of the most consequential changes in the style of the game since Babe Ruth's impact on baseball in 1920.

Prior to 1974 pitchers were expected to come to a pause before delivering a pitch. A pause could be anything from a momentary hesitation to a much longer freeze. The intent of the pause requirement was to eliminate the quick pitch, a pitch thrown before the batter was settled in the batter's box. A quick pitch, however, at worst, was a nonpitch with no penalty. Although it was the hitter's responsibility to be alert when stepping into the batter's box, the umpires protected the hitters on quick pitches. Al Lopez tells of such an event:

> I was catching Tom Zachary one day when he quick pitched a hitter. Bill Klem was umpiring behind the plate. He jumped to one side, arms in the air, hollering, "No pitch!" Then he called Zachary to the plate.

"Young man," he said, "let's not have any more of those quick pitches. A hitter might not be looking. You wouldn't want to hit him, would you?" There was no balk, no ball, no nothing. Today the quick pitch is a balk, but I don't remember it ever being called in the old days.

In 1974, the National League and its umpires reinterpreted the balk rule. The new interpretation shifted the emphasis to a primary concern with the base runners. The quick pitch was now a balk advancing the base runners as well as a nonpitch for the hitter. That change in itself was no particular problem for anyone. What became far more troubling and which initiated radical changes in the style of the game was the sudden, obsessive attention by the umpires to the pitchers' moves to first base.

In 1974, the umpires, particularly in the National League, began to nitpick the pitchers' moves to first base. Was the move a straightforward throw, or was there a wiggle by the pitcher's leg, his shoulder or his head, with the intent to deceive the runner? To the umpires any such gestures, however slight, were now interpreted as an improper intent to confuse the base runner and therefore a balk. Each of the four umpires was empowered to make the balk call without any consensus of opinion. Any umpire could call a balk even though none of the remaining three umpires detected any infraction. In that one year, 1974, the National League umpires called a record-breaking 140 balks. This was more than two and one-half times as many as the 52 balks in the preceding year. The American League umpires who had a lukewarm interest in this new trend showed a modest increase in balk calls. The compatibility in balks that existed between the leagues in previous years vanished in 1974. From 1974 through 1987 the National League umpires kept up their intensity, reaching a new record of 219 balks in 1987. During that 13-year span, they called three times as many balks as in the preceding 13 years, and twice as many balks as the American League umpires. There is no valid reason for any disparity in the number of balks between two leagues.

With the National League umpires' zeal in calling balks, the pitchers, understandably, became tentative in their moves to first. The skills they developed in containing base runners were now a liability and a risk. As a result, base runners became more daring, taking leads off first base to the edge of the cut-out area and even onto the grass. We're talking about 12- to 15-foot leads, about twice as much as in the years prior to 1974.

The focus of the game shifted to the running game with base stealing as the game's most potent offensive weapon. "Singles" hitters, especially those with blazing speed, have become the most productive forces on their ball clubs, creating havoc on the bases by putting relentless pressure on pitchers, catchers, and infielders. For them a single or a walk is followed by a routine steal of second base, the equivalent of a double. Often the catcher's throw ends in the outfield with the runner advancing to third.

What prompted the umpires to tinker with the balk rule in 1974? It appears that the change in the interpretation of the rule was a unilateral decision of the National League umpires.

Buzzie Bavasi made this observation: "The reinterpretation of the balk rule in 1974 may have originated in the league offices, although I doubt it. Most likely it was the umpires' idea. I know that none of the owners participated in that decision."

As is often the case, serious repercussions develop from seemingly innocuous beginnings. In earlier years, umpires were content to be invisible participants in the game, avoiding controversy as a matter of policy. That attitude changed in the past 15 years. Today, the umpires appear as performers searching for an act. Under the four-umpire system, umpires have contracted an ailment that has become endemic to their profession—ennui.

The four-umpire system is baseball's version of featherbedding.

One would be hard pressed to find a profession that requires as little activity as umpiring on the bases. By rediscovering the balk rule, the umpires found a partial remedy. The balk rule now supplies them with some work and, importantly to them, with a bit of recognition and drama that had previously eluded them. There is a mystique about calling a balk that endows umpires with a status that sets them above all the participants. They are now center stage in situations that are rarely disputed, inasmuch as no manager, pitcher, or even an umpire such as Ron Luciano can recognize the balk infractions. For better or for worse, the umpires' obsession with balk calls has changed the style of the game.

The Table below reveals the dramatic increase in balk calls and stolen bases from the time the rule was reinterpreted in 1974.

BALKS AND STOLEN BASES
(Number of A.L. teams adjusted to conform with N.L.)

	A.L.	N.L.
Balks per Year		
1960–73*	41	48
1974–87**	77	157
Stolen Base per Year		
1960–73*	729	766
1974–87**	1294	1606

*1963 excluded (see below).
**1981 strike year excluded.

The year 1963 produced an aberration in the number of balks and was thus excluded from the computations. It was another example of the anomalies in baseball—the exercise of rigid traditionalism combined with off-the-wall experimentation. That was the year when the National League, at the not so altruistic urging of Walter O'Malley of the Los Angeles Dodgers, decided to tinker with the balk rule by introducing the "one-second" regulation.

This O'Malley proposal required pitchers to come to a minimum one-second stop before delivering a pitch from a set position. One second—not a moment less! The penalty for an infraction was a balk.

In previous years, the balk rules gave pitchers a latitude ranging from a momentary pause to a 20-second interval before delivering a pitch. Under the O'Malley directive, umpires had to mentally calculate and synchronize, with 100 percent accuracy, a stop of at least 1 second before the delivery of a pitched ball. The American League wisely ignored O'Malley's ignoble experiment. In the National League, however, O'Malley's domain, the umpires struggled with an impossible task. With any of the four umpires privileged to call a balk, and with no hope of consistency among the umpires in precisely measuring the interval of a "second," balk calls were flying from all sources. As reported in baseball's Official Guide, by May 7, in a period of one month, "the balk count stood at 96, in the National League." The National League, alone, called more balks in the first *30 days* of 1963, than the *total* number of balks in *both* leagues in any prior *year* in baseball's history!

In one month's time, a "one-second" bit of meshugaas stopped baseball's historical clock, virtually bringing the game to its knees. Referring to one unfortunate pitcher, the Guide stated that Bob Friend of the Pittsburgh Pirates "was charged with six [balks] in his first two outings, equaling the previous major league record for a *season*. Further, "with the pitchers, managers and brass all squawking," and the media and fans disgusted with the destruction of the subtle and hallowed rhythms of the game, the O'Malley dictate was quickly canceled by the National League. After one month's chaos, a semblance of balance and sanity was restored to the game. The year ended with 147 balks called in the National League—the largest number of balks in a season, to that time. The American League posted a modest 47 balks.

O'Malley's motivation was his desire to promote and protect

his star attraction, Maury Wills, the Dodgers' shortstop. Wills set the major league stolen-base record the year before, compiling an astonishing 104 stolen bases. Apparently, in the last part of that 1962 season, pitchers began to convert to a no-windup pitching style in an effort to curb Wills' base-stealing success. It is unclear how no-windup pitching could have any effect on stolen-base attempts. Evidently, O'Malley's suspicions were aroused. He saw something no one else did. The rest is history.

For unknown reasons that have mystified players, managers, fans, and the media, more changes in the balk rule were introduced into the 1988 season. This was not a case of reinterpreting the 1974 rule. This involved new attitudes and new language in the balk rule. The pause that pitchers previously used was no longer acceptable. New words—"a discernible stop"—were substituted. Although a pause is commonly defined as "a cessation of activity," it is apparent that with baseball umpires, as in *Alice in Wonderland*, words mean only what the users intend them to mean.

The balk rule, as now interpreted, has introduced an unbridled interference in the rhythms of the game and has destroyed much of the suspense and drama in baseball. For example, a potential base-stealer who reaches first base in a close game gives rise to dramatic confrontations that put the fans as well as the players on edge. That situation elicits the highest skills of the players and the best judgment of the managers.

The pitcher and the base runner become locked in a pivotal duel. The pitcher and his catcher must be particularly careful in their selection of pitches to the plate. A breaking ball could be a problem. It's a slower pitch than a fastball, harder for the catcher to handle, and thus easier for the base runner to steal a base. If a fastball is thrown, then the advantage is given to the hitter.

The infielders are similarly involved. They are concerned with the possibility of a hit-and-run play as well as a straight steal. For either eventuality, they must position themselves closer to the bag, thus opening larger holes in the infields.

The managers are also engaged in a combat of competing strategies. When does one manager call for the steal or the hit and run? And when does the opposing manager counter with a pitchout?

Another example of a suspenseful situation: A runner on third base in a one-run game. Will the hitter be able to drive in that important run? Is there a possibility of a squeeze play?

Enter the umpires. *Balk!* The balloon is punctured. Suspense and drama are dissipated. The runner on first ambles to second. Or the runner on third scores the tying run. The outcome of the game was not determined by a pitch or hit. Neither the skills of the players nor the sagacity of the managers won or lost the battle. The end result has been decided by the intrusion of an imprecise, unnecessary technicality.

The umpires' obsession with the balk rule has taken the game out of the hands of the performers and has diminished the fans' enjoyment of the game. The dubious value of the "discernible stop" provision may assuage the need of baseball's overly officious Rules Committee for power and recognition and may feed the burgeoning egos of the umpires. But it would be surprising to find a single player, manager, member of the media, or fan who sees any value in this fixation with the balk rule.

The year 1988 will have produced an ignominious record number of balks. The lesson of 1963 has not been learned.

12 Computerball Statistics Are Bullshit!

"I really don't care much about baseball or looking at ball games. All my interest is in statistics."
—Ernie Lanigan, old-time statistician, quoted in
The Hidden Game of Baseball, by Thorn and Palmer.

Perhaps it was all Jacques Barzun's fault, when he said: "Whoever would learn the heart and mind of America had better learn baseball."

He should have added the caveat: "However, don't go messing around with computerball statistics. You may end up knowing everything about numbers but nothing about baseball."

Computerball statistics are not like the familiar and comprehensible statistics that appear in the sport pages of the daily press and comprise habitual reading material for millions of fans. These day-to-day tabulations are a harmless addiction that keep the fans posted on the standings in the pennant race, the averages of their favorite players, the rivalries in home runs and stolen bases, and a variety of similar details. Yet such statistics do not dominate the fans' interests to the exclusion of the basic pleasures they get from attending ball games. Fans enjoy the traditional features of baseball, the opening ceremonies, the distinctive styles and mannerisms of the players, the seventh-inning stretch, and even the disputes. These conventional statistics are intended only as fodder to be digested and enjoyed by the baseball public, and for use by the media. The statisticians who provide such information are content to let the public and the media draw their own conclusions as to the meaning, if any, of their statistics. They do not project strategies for the players, managers, and baseball executives, based upon their statistics. They recognize that statistics are after-the-fact data that have no value in designing how the game should be played.

Not so with the New Statisticians. They are the disciples of the Ernest Lanigan approach to baseball. Their game is computerball, a game that is played in mainframe monsters, not on the ball field. It involves the accumulation of masses of statistics, which are shaped into convoluted theories. Their data are spiced with incomprehensible formulas, equations, Pythagorean principles, coefficients, and arcane hypotheses—from all of which they attempt to evaluate the skills of major league players from as far back as the 1880s. They set themselves up as the final authorities on the strategies of the game. They presume to tell us who are the "best players of today and all-time" . . . "what Ty Cobb would hit today" . . . "what [George] Brett would hit in 1920," and similar divine truths. They know all there is to know about baseball except for one fact—computerball statistics are bullshit!

To some New Statisticians, such as Thorn and Palmer in their book *The Hidden Game,* the traditional statistics need to be restructured, with new formulations "plumbing the meaning of numbers." They espouse a "utopian zero-sum system in which every action by the offense has a corresponding and inverse action in the defense and everything balances in the end." As they see it, "the lure for baseball statisticians is that the mathematical universe in which the game is played can be fully comprehended." They favor the theories of "The Pythagoreans and the Cabalists," to whom "numbers are at the core of creation." Who can fathom this meshugaas?

The basic problem with the New Statisticians is they see baseball as a science and not as an art. They fail to recognize that there is not an iota of science in the play and management of a baseball game, not a single statistic that can be useful in the vagaries of game conditions. Inferences can be drawn from statistics, but inferences do not compute into facts.

Baseball is not a game played by robots who can be programmed to perform with predictable results. Baseball players are subject to the capriciousness that is inherent in all professional sports. Baseball involves human errors, physical and mental; hot streaks and slumps; good breaks and bad breaks—all combined with the artistry of its performers. Baseball relies upon the intuitive judgments of its managers, coaches, and players. There is an ebb and flow in every ball game which involves moves and counter-moves, nuances and subtleties that can be seen, understood, and enjoyed—but never statistically calculated or predicted.

For example, the computerball statisticians seem particularly concerned with Ty Cobb's lifetime .367 average. What would Cobb hit if his career took place in the seventies and eighties? No one can possibly have that answer. The question of whether Cobb would hit .367 or as one statistician has determined, .289 or some figure in between, as projected by others, misses the point. Such determinations cannot reflect the full extent of Ty Cobb's skill. They cannot measure Cobb's techniques, what he did when on base, the effect he had on the pitchers and infielders, and how he influenced the outcome of a game by tactics and intimidation.

I don't recall any discussion with an old-timer in which Ty Cobb's .367 average was mentioned. Ossie Bluege discussed Cobb from a much broader view:

> Cobb could beat you in so many ways. When he was at bat, the infield would shorten up. I would be two or three steps closer to the plate, to protect against the bunt, but this would make it easier for Cobb to hit sharp drives by me. When he was on base, the shortstop and second baseman were a step or two closer to the bag to make the double play before Cobb could get to them. We could never relax when playing

against him. The pitchers were often jittery and less effective when Cobb was on base, because they never knew what he'd do next. He'd steal home if the pitcher wasn't alert, and often caused them to balk by making fake attempts to steal home.

How many games did Cobb win by his daring on the bases? How many rallies did he prolong, and what was the value of the psychological stress he imposed upon pitchers and infielders? How can statisticians place statistical ratings on these features of Ty Cobb's play?

Jackie Robinson was a comparable example. His batting statistics were not overwhelming, and he hardly rated among the most outstanding defensive players in baseball's history. But he too was an intimidator on the bases. He put pressure on the opposition, compelling defensive changes in their play. He made the infielders move closer to the bags, thus producing larger holes in the infield. To prevent Robinson from stealing bases, pitchers were compelled to alter their natural deliveries and their selection of pitches. All of this favored the hitters on his club. In effect, Robinson, as with Ty Cobb, could win games through tactics. Players such as Vince Coleman, Rickey Henderson, Juan Samuel, Tim Raines, and Eric Davis are some of many current-day intimidators. As with Cobb and Robinson, they possess values that cannot be measured statistically.

The vacuity of statistics is often apparent in game situations. For example, on what basis does a third-base coach send or not send a runner to the plate? Statisticians may calculate the odds of a runner trying to score from second base on a line drive single against Dave Winfield's arm. Yet the coach is concerned with more mundane considerations. Is Winfield out of position? Is he backing up on the hit or coming forward? Is he handling the ball cleanly? What are the ground conditions? Even if every factor is favorable for Winfield, the gamble may still be worthwhile if there are two outs in a one-run game and the runner was off with the hit.

Conversely, the same coach might hold up a runner at third base against an outfielder with a poor arm—if there are less than two outs; if the ball is sharply hit; or if it's fielded on one bounce with the outfielder moving rapidly forward in good throwing position. These split-second decisions are intuitive and are not motivated by statistics or percentages.

None of these shadings of baseball can be tabulated statistically. The fan who can understand the reasoning for the strategies, decisions, and activities on the ball field, will have learned more about baseball than he could in years of fiddling around with statistical abstractions.

Thorn and Palmer claim that their computers can provide "a true picture of the mathematical aspects of the game." What they fail to recognize is that these "true pictures" are nothing more than after-the-fact bookkeeping. They admit that major league managers such as George Bamberger and Dick Williams "have forgotten more baseball than we will ever know." But that shortcoming doesn't slow them from challenging and imposing their judgments on these managers, and upon all other managers and the executives who operate the baseball franchises. They claim:

> . . .Managers talk about playing by The Book but they've never even *read* The Book. They don't know what's in it. They all use the same old strategies, many of which are ridiculous. Every mathematical analysis shows that the intentional walk is almost always a bad play, stolen bases are only marginally useful, and the sacrifice bunt is a useless vestige of the deadball era when they didn't pinch-hit for pitchers.

It would be hard to find a paragraph in any book on baseball that contains more inaccuracies and more presumptuousness than the above statement. These New Statisticians attribute to major league managers an affinity for playing by "The Book." Yet no one has ever heard a major league manager ever make a reference to any such literature. They know that there is no manager's "book," never has been, and never will be.

There isn't and can't be a standard method of baseball strategy among managers. A baseball game is too complex to be standardized. Managerial styles are shaped by the talents of the players, their strengths and their weaknesses. All managers prefer a set lineup of complete, every-day players. But that is an ideal, not a reality. Many players are one dimensional. Some can hit but can't field. Others can field and run but lack hitting ability and power. Some are effective against right-handed pitching and helpless against left-handers.

Chuck Tanner, manager of the Atlanta club, is quoted in Thorn and Palmer's book: "Don't let stats get in your way of judgment. Figures don't always tell the truth. I'd rather use good judgment than cold stats."

The authors responded: "Who's saying stats are antithetical to good judgment or common sense? . . . We have shown that by analyzing events of all kinds in terms of their run-scoring potential and win probability, aided by the computer, the percentages [stats] need not be a matter of debate."

Statistics may not necessarily be antithetical to "good judgment or common sense," but statistics are totally irrelevant on the ball field. That's what Chuck Tanner was trying to get across, and what these statisticians do not perceive. They say "the percentages need not be a matter of debate." Yet that is the essence of the game *they* play, which is nothing more than another form of Hot Stove League baseball. Instead of verbal skirmishes around a wood-burning stove, their game is played in the arena of computerized polemics.

The computerball statisticians are not daunted. They find the answers to baseball problems in such equations as:

$$P_b \times V_s + (1 - P_b) \times V_f = V_p$$

Now there's a formula for managerial success that would have appealed to Casey Stengel, Leo Durocher, Yogi Berra, and Billy Martin. Unfortunately, managers insist on styling their game upon their experience. It's amazing how the game has survived without resorting to equations, Pythagorean principles, or Cabalistic theories.

Thorn and Palmer exult over the brilliance of a fellow statistician who recorded such monumental data as "a bloop single over first base off a right-handed pitcher, traveling 135 feet." Presumably, it is the ball, not the pitcher, that is being propelled 135 feet into right field. Thorn and Palmer tell us this is an example of the data that a computer "can easily store and later retrieve." That may be a priceless bit of information—but how can it be used? They have that answer, too:

> By storing play-by-play data for future analysis, the computer permits managers to keep track of how individual batters fare against individual pitchers and vice versa, or how players perform under a myriad of varying conditions, day vs. night, artificial turf vs. grass, curve ball vs. fastball, etc.

Now, all we need is to assemble the major league managers and show them how simple their jobs would be if statistical strategy could be programmed for them. These statisticians maintain that the managers could use the computer "before and after games, for information storage and retrieval, for situational stats, for strategy analysis, for evaluating prospective roster changes." Sounds good. But why stop there? Why not obtain a rule change so that a statistician could sit alongside of a manager, poised behind a computer, working keyboard symbols and providing instant strategy to relieve the brain strain on his beleaguered associate.

No statistician is more addicted to analyzing the talents of players through obtuse theories than Bill James. In his annual *Bill James Baseball Abstract*, he graciously acknowledges that he is "something less than a world-class scientist." He refers to himself as a "sabermetrician." I can't tell you what that means. I don't know. He insists that he does not rely upon statistical analysis as much as upon "Pythagorean methods" and his "compelling logic." He includes in his calculations such esoteric factors as climatic conditions, ball park configurations, and the moods and birthdays of players. His vantage point of observing baseball is from the "outside," so that he can obtain a "perspective" of the game without the intrusion of the "routines and the boredom of baseball's life-style." To him the perspective of baseball is best achieved "only when the details are lost." Presumably, the farther one gets away from baseball the more one can learn about the game.

Thorn and Palmer pay homage to Bill James for having "converted thousands to his view that errors don't count for much anymore." Evidently through Mr. James's "compelling logic" and their statistical analyses, it is OK to give an opposing team more than three outs in an inning. Can Thorn, Palmer, or James, produce one professional in baseball, one sports writer, or even an average fan who will agree with that absurdity?

The typical Bill James approach in his yearly *Abstract* is to deny the obvious and promote the outrageous. He concedes that he has "probably developed 30 to 40 formulas, most of them obsolete." He admits "that there are many basic, fundamental facets of baseball" of which he has "little knowledge" and with which he "cannot deal."

What is interesting about Bill James is his appetite for the bizarre. He is not a statistician in the manner of Thorn and Palmer or the contributors to their book, *The Hidden Game of Baseball.* Yet he borrows from their research while admitting its lack of value. He manages to touch all bases, sometimes in reverse order. In his *Baseball Abstract* he admits:

> . . . The ratings of ball players is an arrogant bit of nonsense, . . . [and] I
> am very leery of . . . statistics which consider everything and provide
> the once and final answer to great baseball questions like: who was
> the greatest player ever? or who really belongs in the Hall of Fame? . . . It
> is my considered opinion that we have no business answering these
> questions by formula. . . . The search for great statistics . . . is not and
> cannot be a scientific undertaking. . . . Great statistics have no idea
> of what they are measuring. . . . People should understand that when
> I say opinions are bullshit, it is not other people's opinions that I'm
> referring to. I don't value my own opinions. . . . I take the various me-
> thods that I have developed to measure different things, and I combine
> them as best I can.

His quotes will get no argument from me or from any professional in baseball. Yet these quotes don't square with his books.
It's as if different people with different convictions concocted his
baseball abstract. He adjures computerball statistics but sponsors
their theories. He acknowledges the "compelling logic" of his
studies, predictions, and evaluations of teams and players, yet applies farfetched and illogical factors in arriving at his conclusions.

One of his most curious methods was a study of the influence
of biorhythms on the performance of baseball players. This theory
apparently involves inherent intellectual and emotional cycles.
He studied the biorhythmic cycles of 11 players, from which he
concluded that "some of the players did indeed perform much
better when on a triple high, than when on a triple low." Sort
of a baseball menopause.

What sustains the latter-day Ernest Lanigans is their addiction
to their computerized analysis. They are enamored of lists, such
as Thorn and Palmer's compilation of the 140 "best players" and
"best pitchers" in baseball's history. For example, they rank Norm
Cash as the 75th greatest player in the history of the game. He
is rated as a better player than all of the following: Richie Ashburn,
Ernie Banks, Sam Crawford, Goose Goslin, Harry Heilmann,

Charlie Keller, Ralph Kiner, Chuck Klein, Brooks Robinson, Al Simmons, George Sisler, Duke Snider, Bill Terry, and Zack Wheat. Does any fan believe that? They rate "Dizzy" Trout as the 30th greatest pitcher in the history of baseball. He is rated as a better pitcher than all of the following: Tommy Bridges, Red Faber, Bob Feller, Wes Ferrell, Carl Mays, Eddie Plank, Rube Waddell, Juan Marichal, Robin Roberts, Red Ruffing, Bucky Walters, Sandy Koufax, Dizzy Dean, Nolan Ryan, Mort Cooper, Early Wynn, Lefty Gomez, Allie Reynolds, Dazzy Vance, and Rube Marquard. Who besides these statisticians would believe that foolishness?

These New Statisticians are particularly smitten with their "On Base Average" (OBA) statistic. How important is this OBA statistic? To them, it is of major importance. They claim that their OBA ratings are "a better measure of hitting ability . . . than batting averages." They admit they've been waiting for "twenty-five to thirty years" for "official" adoption of that statistic. But they are patient. "We will wait our turn," they say.

It may come as a shock to them, but it would take a professional, or a reasonably well-versed fan, about 25 to 30 seconds to see why their OBA ratings are not accurate measurements of the talent of players. Let's try a scenario.

Although you've been a baseball fan for many years, you are now in the role of either a general manager or a field manager of a major league club. Your club owns the contracts of the following list of 54 players, in their prime. Many of these players you've seen in action. The others may have played before your time, but you know of them by their reputations and through reports from reliable major league sources. Forty-eight of your players are in the Hall of Fame. The 6 others will certainly enter that select company when eligible. These are your 54 players:

Mel Ott	Mickey Cochrane	Joe Sewell
Rod Carew	Mike Schmidt	George Sisler
Arky Vaughan	Eddie Mathews	Duke Snider
Jimmie Foxx	Ralph Kiner	Pie Traynor
Frank Robinson	Hank Greenberg	Lloyd Waner
Honus Wagner	Joe DiMaggio	Zack Wheat
Chick Hafey	Pete Rose	Peewee Reese
Nap Lajoie	Eddy Murray	Brooks Robinson
Ross Youngs	Carl Yastrzemski	Joe Medwick
Johnny Mize	Hack Wilson	Joe Cronin
Earle Combs	Harmon Killebrew	Gabby Hartnett
Willie Mays	Paul Waner	Billy Herman
Jackie Robinson	Luke Appling	Harry Hooper
Harry Heilmann	Bill Terry	Travis Jackson
Willie McCovey	Heinie Manush	Kiki Cuyler
Hank Aaron	Edd Roush	Bill Dickey
Al Kaline	Goose Goslin	Al Simmons
George Brett	Charlie Gehringer	Frankie Frisch

Question. Would you trade any one of your players for any one of the following: Gene Tenace, Mike Hargrove, Bernie Carbo, Merv Rettemund, Don Buford, Norm Cash, or Bill North?

You would not? According to the computerball statisticians, there is something wrong with your judgment. These "experts" rate Gene Tenace and Mike Hargrove higher than *all* of your 54 players. That's right. Gene Tenace and Mike Hargrove rate as numbers 15 and 16 among the 100 greatest players in all of baseball's history, based on their OBA formula. Carbo rates higher than 51 of your players; Rettemund higher than 49; Buford higher than 47 players; Cash is better than 46; and Bill North tops 45 players. In fact 15 Hall of Fame players—Cuyler, Frisch, Hafey, Hartnett, Billy Herman, Hooper, Travis Jackson, Manush, Medwick, Roush, Joe Sewell, Sisler, Simmons, Traynor, and Wheat— don't even rate in the first 100.

Do the statisticians really believe that any knowledgeable fan, let alone a professional, would rate the talent of 54 of the greatest players in history behind 7 journeymen, in any category of baseball?

In compiling their OBA statistic, Thorn and Palmer added walks and times hit by pitches to the base hits achieved by hitters. Under that formula, a walk to Tenace or Hargrove is the equivalent of a base hit by players such as Hank Greenberg, Joe DiMaggio, Willie Mays, George Sisler, or Bill Terry. These statisticians, in their OBA calculations, apparently do not consider the value of extra base hits, baserunning, and scoring runs. Nor do they comprehend that walks can be a liability as well as an asset.

There are at least three types of "walks" in baseball. Walks to exceptional hitters such as Babe Ruth or Ted Williams were in the intentional category. Pitchers were instructed *never* to give Babe Ruth a good ball to hit, *never* to throw him a strike with men on base. He was even walked *intentionally* with the bases loaded. And what's more, it was sound strategy. Pitchers never pitch carelessly to good hitters, especially to power hitters. They pitch around them. They prefer to walk such hitters rather than give them a good ball to hit.

Power hitters, such as Babe Ruth, were often swinging at pitches that were out of the strike zone, especially with men on base. They couldn't afford to be "choosy" when there were runners waiting to score. And being quality hitters, they were not especially handicapped by pitches that were slightly off the mark. They disdained walks. When they were walked, it was by the design of the pitchers.

Pitchers also pitched "around" the plate to Williams, to avoid giving him a good ball to hit. But unlike other exceptional hitters, Williams would not—in fact, could not—bring himself to swing at a pitch that was even a fraction of an inch out of the strike

147

zone. No doubt every one of his managers often agonized over Williams' refusal to swing at pitches that were marginally off the plate. He would draw walks when he undoubtedly could have driven in runs by swinging at pitches that were not strikes. But it's hard to fault Williams' judgment. He was so disciplined as a hitter that he could not swing at bad pitches without breaking down his perfect batting style. He had a valid point. Once he started swinging at pitches that were off the plate, where would it stop? He would be continually enlarging the pitchers' strike zone and would ultimately become less effective as a hitter.

Another type of walk is the walk to lead-off men, whose objective is to get on base for other hitters to drive them home. The most dangerous lead-off men are the premier base stealers. To them, a walk is the equivalent of an extra base hit. They raise hell with the defense. Their walks are exceptional assets.

The least-understood type of walk—and what distorts the OBA statistics—is the walk to players who should not be taking walks. Pitchers do not pitch around them. Pitchers throw strikes to them, but these hitters don't make contact. These are the "Gene Tenace" type of hitter. They are positioned in the batting order to drive in runs, but they can't. They take strikes. They can't hit a curveball. They keep fouling off pitches that should be hit into fair territory, scoring runners. They spend an inordinate amount of time at the plate, inducing a volume of pitches that eventually brings them to a 3-and-2 count. From then on, it's often a walk or a strikeout. They leave an excessive number of runners on base. Their walks are liabilities, not assets. Tenace may be rated as number 16 among the greatest OBA hitters in the history of the game—but he is also number 11 on the all-time list of strikeouts per times at bat. It is a reasonable assumption that players such as Tenace and Hargrove, who would take pitch after pitch without swinging or making contact, have achieved more 3-and-2 counts and spent more minutes at the plate per times at bat than any other players in history.

Hank Greenberg once described the difference between a good hitter and a bad hitter in this way: "A good hitter, when he gets his 'pay' ball, does something positive with it. A bad hitter will hit a foul ball off such pitches."

It is useless to attempt to comprehend the calculations of these statisticians. It is simpler to examine their conclusions. They hold George Sisler and Bill Terry in low esteem. It has something to do with Sisler and Terry not getting enough walks, in comparison with players such as Tenace, Hargrove, and Cash. Of course, while these three were accumulating walks, Sisler and Terry were compiling base hits, averaging over 200 hits a year. That doesn't impress the statisticians. They maintain that those .400 averages "were not enough to post impressive OBAs. . . . Sisler and Terry were turning up their noses at walks with the intent of maximizing extra base hits—nope, these were relatively soft batting averages, more like Mickey Rivers or Willie Wilson. . . ." You see, even a .400 average can't impress them. It fouls up their theories.

Boggles the mind, doesn't it? How could Sisler and Terry pile up walks when they were, instead, amassing base hits? Isn't a hit more important than a walk? How could Sisler's and Terry's averages be "soft" if they were "maximizing extra base hits"?

It is regrettable that Bill Veeck's midget, Eddie Gaedel, was prohibited from pursuing his major league career. By going into a crouch, Gaedel would have offered a six-inch strike zone, an impossible target for the pitchers. Assume that he obeyed Bill Veeck's order, "*Never* swing at a pitch. I'm up there on the roof with a rifle. You make one pass at a ball and you're *dead!*" Gaedel could have set an all-time record for walks and would have had the number-one OBA rating in all of baseball's history.

Thorn and Palmer set up their "Pantheon" of Hall of Famers.

They don't like many of the players enshrined in Cooperstown, particularly those Hall of Famers who played in the twenties and thirties. They prefer players such as Norm Cash, who had but 1 exceptional year in 17 years. He had a lot of walks, as well as an impressive number of strikeouts. His walks overwhelm the statisticians. Hargrove, Tenace, and Cash are favored for their Hall of Fame Pantheon. Thus, in their Pantheon you will not find any of the following players from the 1920s and 1930s: Earl Averill, Jim Bottomley, Max Carey, Earle Combs, Kiki Cuyler, Chick Hafey, Harry Hooper, Travis Jackson, Fred Lindstrom, Heinie Manush, Sam Rice, Edd Roush, Ray Schalk, Pie Traynor, Lloyd Waner, Hack Wilson, Ross Youngs, and pitchers Dizzy Dean, Lefty Gomez, Jesse Haines, Waite Hoyt, and Eppa Rixey.

They also eliminate more modern Hall of Famers, such as Roy Campanella, George Kell, Sandy Koufax, and Early Wynn.

These players are replaced in their pantheon by Bobby Bonds, Cesar Cedeno, Ron Cey, Darrell Evans, Roy Smalley, Reggie Smith, Rusty Staub, Dick Allen, Rocky Colavito, Ron Santo, Jim Wynn, among others.

The New Statisticians place a low value on defense. To them defense represents only "six percent of the game," even though all professionals in baseball insist that defense plays a major and vital role in success. With the help of Bill James, the statisticians claim to have developed a system of determining the best defensive players in baseball's history. Bill James's contribution is what he calls the "Range Factor." Apparently, from his position on the "outside" of baseball, he can gauge those players with the most range in the field. Thorn and Palmer add to the "Range Factor" with their own specialty—the Linear Weights System. I haven't the slightest idea what that entails.

By combining their theories, these authorities presume to tell us which players were the lifetime best in their positions defensively, which were underrated, and which were overrated. They urge readers to "distrust your senses, have faith in the instruments." Presumably they mean their computers. Their "instruments" offer us the following meshugaas:

> Notable by their surprisingly indifferent showings . . . are some men universally regarded as all-time greats at their positions . . . Hal Chase, Bobby Richardson, Peewee Reese, Brooks Robinson, Paul Blair and Johnny Bench. Richardson's totals may have been hurt by the preponderance of left-hand pitchers in the Yankees [??]; Reese was renowned for his reliability more than his range; and Robinson and Blair, well, they won Gold Gloves . . . despite evidence . . . that other were doing the job more effectively. . . . Robinson and Blair *looked good* [their emphasis, not mine] . . . which is the way to win Gold Gloves, alas.

Their instruments further tell us that Richie Ashburn, admittedly a good outfielder, "saved more runs in the outfield than anyone except Max Carey and Tris Speaker. Mays and DiMaggio weren't even close."

That statement probably embarrasses Ashburn more than anyone else. No mention of Paul Blair. He isn't listed among the good outfielders. Brooks Robinson is ranked defensively 25 spots behind Ron Cey and Darrell Evans. Cey is also rated as superior in defense to Marty Marion, Joe Gordon, Gary Templeton, Dave Concepcion, and Ken Boyer. Bump Wills is considered better than Billy Herman, Travis Jackson, Nellie Fox, and Roy McMillan. Charlie Gehringer and Willie Kamm receive no recognition among the good infielders. The statisticians assure us that "it was so." But despite their pleas to "distrust your senses, have faith in the instruments," there are fans and professionals who prefer to believe their eyes.

The statisticians' conclusions on the rating of pitchers are equally enlightening. They tell us: "Strikeouts are an overrated indicator of pitching ability. . . . The strikeout is romantic, glamorous—a pitcher's opportunity to do something all by himself, unaided by his fielders."

Thus, good-bye to Walter Johnson, Bob Grove, Bob Feller, Sandy Koufax, Nolan Ryan, Steve Carlton, Tom Seaver, Dwight Gooden, and Mike Scott—you fakers. We might have respected you more if your strikeouts were less.

According to the statisticians, pitchers are supposed to do more than just pitch. They are supposed to hit, too. Thus Sandy Koufax ranks at number 60 on their list of pitchers. He did not hit well enough. The same with Dizzy Dean. Ahead of them we find Phil Niekro (12), Bert Blyleven (23), Tommy John (28), and Steve Rogers (48). Eight other Hall of Famers, besides Koufax and Dizzy Dean, are dropped from Hall of Fame status. Nolan Ryan is 107 on their list. If Koufax and Ryan could only have spent their careers in the American League, with its designated hitters, they might have achieved greater recognition from these "experts." To hard-throwing strikeout pitchers, we offer this bit of advice: Do something about your hitting. You can see what's happened to Koufax and Ryan despite their strikeouts, shutouts, and no-hitters. Your strikeouts, your shutouts, and even your no-hitters will get lost in the shuffle unless you pick up your hitting or switch to the American League.

The statisticians are not through. They have more to offer than mere determination of the best hitters, the best defensive players, and the best pitchers throughout baseball's history. They don't overlook guiding the managers. Through their computerball analyses, they construct the ideal batting orders. And for the front-office executives, they have the solution on how to operate their ball clubs successfully. They are particularly solicitous of the New York Yankees. The following are some of their previous recommendations: "Upgrade first base, [by dumping] Mattingly. He doesn't draw enough walks or hit with enough power." [Twenty-three home runs in 1984 didn't satisfy them.]

Retain Steve Kemp—a proven quantity. [Sorry, men, but this "proven quantity" was traded to Pittsburgh and flailed away at a .200 pace.] "Trade Guidry and Righetti, [even though] the fans would scream." [More likely they would tear down the ball park.] And as a final suggestion, "pick up a right hand starter or two—Dave Stieb would be nice."

To show that they don't play favorites, they are willing to assist the remaining 25 major league clubs by giving them "a complete statistical line—in the manner shown above for the Yankees." That's what mucking about with statistics can do to nice people.

Wouldn't it be more sensible to accept the following approach to baseball as expressed by a certain "authority"?

Statistics . . . consume knowledge, but don't yield it. . . . There is no way in the world to evolve a set of standards which is as comprehensive, as complex, as fair or as open to improvement, as is human judgment. There are simply too many things in the game of baseball which are not measured, are poorly measured, and are still in the process of being measured.

Who said that? None other than Bill James. We finally agree.

In the years prior to World War II baseball was notable for its resistance to change. Actually there was little demand for changes in baseball. With the exceptions of the Federal League raids in 1914 and the Black Sox scandal in 1919, baseball was a placid business, unruffled by serious problems in those early years. The men who conducted the affairs of baseball consisted of former players and managers, such as Charles Comiskey, Clark Griffith, and Connie Mack, and 13 other club owners who were geared to the conditions of the times. Some of these men had been in the game from the turn of the century. They were the dinosaurs of baseball.

The entrance of Judge Landis as baseball's commissioner after the "Black Sox" scandal coincided with the emergence of Babe Ruth, who became game's most dominant player. These two were responsible for the most significant changes in baseball from 1920 to the end of the war years in 1945. Landis did his part by guiding baseball through the after-shocks of the scandal and restoring its integrity. Babe Ruth changed the style of the game with his long-ball hitting and generated increased attendance and greater gate receipts, which consequently forced some of the owners to make their most important financial decision—expansion of their ball parks.

For most of the owners, these single-purpose pieces of real estate and their baseball franchises represented their entire wealth and only source of income. They were understandably cautious about decisions that involved outlays of what were to them enormous sums of money. Some owners, such as William Wrigley, and Jake Ruppert, had large business investments outside of baseball. Yet despite the disparity in wealth, the 16 club owners were a tight-knit group with one cause in common. When it came to player salaries, it was "hold the line."

The owners had the leverage, and they used it. The reserve clause in the player contacts, which bound a player to his club in perpetuity, was a standard provision that was tested in the courts and upheld. A player had to accept an owner's final salary offer or an owner's decision to sell or trade the player to another ball club. The player's option was to sit it out, which some of them did.

During the Depression years in the 1930s, there were extenuating circumstances for many of the club owners in their tight-fisted treatment of the players. Attendance was dropping, and there were no profits, only losses. Unlike his more affluent counterparts, Connie Mack had no cash reserves to keep him from bankruptcy. His only recourse was to sell off his best players and reduce his payroll in order to stay alive in the only business he had and knew. He was not alone in this practice during those lean years. Branch Rickey's custom was to sell players for all cash, with no exchange of players. He could afford to do that without weakening his ball club, having a well-established source of young, talented players from his minor league teams. With no minimum salary to contend with, Rickey, as well as all the other major league operators, were signing gifted young players for as little as $600 per month. That was the management style through 1939.

The war years depleted the major league rosters of their players. Every healthy player changed his baseball uniform for the more important military attire. Replacements were assembled from every available source. Long-retired players were making comebacks, and minor leaguers from any level of play were experiencing the once-in-a-lifetime thrill of wearing major league uniforms. Even a one-armed player, Pete Gray, landed an outfield spot on the St. Louis Browns. Until the war ended, it was hit-and-miss baseball, with more miss and less hit.

The postwar years, beginning in 1945, brought to baseball a prosperity never equaled or imagined in any previous time. Yet despite their thriving income, the major league owners could not shed their addiction to the meager player salaries of the prewar years. The cure came quickly. A sleeping giant was awakening, whose footprints would soon make indelible changes in baseball's landscape.

The first step came from a most unlikely source, the Pasquel brothers of Mexico. They detected the discontent of those players who had returned from the war and who were not participating in baseball's newfound prosperity. The Pasquels formed a new league, the Mexican League, initiating raids on the major leagues, enticing players to jump their contracts and head south of the border. The lure, of course, was money, lots of it, in up-front bonuses and salaries, with perks such as the free use of living accommodations for their families. The Mexican League raids soon got the attention of the major leagues, spurring Commissioner Chandler into action. His punishment for the defectors was swift and harsh. He barred the jumpers from organized baseball for five years, which in effect was a lifetime sentence.

In 1946, the Mexican League collapsed. Some players had their penalties commuted by the commissioner. Others remained ineligible for the remainder of their term. Having no other recourse, these expelled players resorted to legal action and prevailed in the courts. Baseball was to pay a big price for its failure to adjust to the changing times.

In the meantime, the most dramatic event in baseball's history occurred in 1947, when Branch Rickey opened the doors to black players, with Jackie Robinson leading the way. The quality of baseball improved as more blacks and Latin players were added to major and minor league rosters, giving the owners another boost in their growing affluence. Baseball was in high gear.

The owners were prospering, but the players were kept out of the process. The rumblings of the players intensified until late in 1947 when the major league players decided to take action. Represented by players Johnny Murphy and Marty Marion and guided by the voluntary efforts of Robert Murphy, an attorney, the players were able to extract from the owners a five-year commitment of $1,000,000 a year to go into a players' pension fund.

In 1952, with Ralph Kiner and Allie Reynolds as spokesmen for the players, these benefits increased substantially. It was not easy. The sessions with the owners involved a walkout by Kiner and Reynolds, who refused to bargain without an attorney at their side. If the major leagues were represented at the bargaining table by several attorneys, why couldn't the players have at least one? The owners finally relented, and J. Norman Lewis became the players' legal representative.

The basic issue was the players' claim to a percentage of the television revenues from the All-Star Game and the World Series. A fixed amount was not acceptable to them. The players also wanted a minimum salary. It took the threat of a players' strike to budge the owners from their hard-set posture. When the contest was over, the players prevailed on both counts. Sixty percent of the TV monies went to the players, and a $5,000 minimum salary was established. In retrospect, it is surprising that the owners would attempt to deny the players the right to be represented by legal counsel, or would contest the moot issue of a modest minimum salary for major league players, or would fail to recognize the validity of the players' right to a fair share of the television revenues that derived solely from attractions provided by the players. These issues set the stage for far more serious problems for the owners in the years ahead.

The precursor of baseball's bag of troubles was the first expansion in 1961, an exercise that reflected the greed of the owners. The American League added 2 franchises, the first break in the 16-team format in the history of the major leagues. Three more expansions followed. By 1977 the major leagues were operating 26 teams, a 60 percent increase.

Expansion served several purposes. It brought huge entry fees, which were shared by the league members. It also permitted the owners to unload upon the newcomers a mixed bag of ineffective players at outrageous prices. These consisted of "name" players, long past their prime, and marginal players—journeymen—who would have been berthed in the minor leagues in previous years. They were major leaguers only by virtue of the uniforms they wore. The limited quality of this talent became a fixed liability that kept the expansion teams mired in the second division, with last place their most familiar position. Expansion, however, had the benefit of providing the existing second-division clubs an opportunity to move up a notch or two in the standings, at the expense of the newcomers.

Although the major league player limit was fixed at 25 players per club, the turnovers on an expansion club sometimes doubled that number. That situation inspired the comment that some clubs had three teams—one on the field, one coming, and one going.

In the meantime, the affairs of baseball were undergoing a shift from its traditional setup of unilateral control by the owners to an unwieldy and lopsided arrangement with the Major League Players Association. On one hand was a group of owners who could not agree among themselves on the simplest issues; they were divided by internal discord, league to league, owner to owner, and owner to commissioner. If the owners were divided and self-defeating the players' union was a model of cohesiveness and resolve. Their 600 plus members were totally united behind the head of their union, Marvin Miller, a highly competent labor leader who became their executive director in 1966.

When push came to shove, the outcome was predictable. The owners caved in. Miller virtually stripped them clean, to the point of overkill. He achieved for the players what the Supreme Court of the United States couldn't give them—free agency. And with that victory, the face of baseball changed forever. In their triumph, the players reaped huge financial rewards. They also brought about the disruption of established teams, disillusionment, resentment, and disgust in the fans and the media, and an unbalanced brand of baseball. But who can blame the players for the excessive salaries?

"If the owners want to overpay us," the players contended, "why should we refuse?" Why indeed?

The right of free agency resulted in a drift of players who raised their level of compensation to almost unbelievable heights. Club owners who were judicious and successful businessmen when operating in the private sector became naive and profligate when operating in the limelight of baseball's public arena. It was a rite of baptism for many club owners. They had to prove to the home-town fans and to the media that they had the sporting blood to compete financially with their fellows for the free-agent players. In the process, players were awarded lavish financial benefits consisting of long-term, even lifetime, contracts; non–interest-bearing loans; prepaid annuities; as well as participation in the private businesses of club owners.

Frequently the beneficiaries of long-term contracts were players of ordinary talent, coming off a single, uncharacteristically successful season. Millions of dollars are still being paid today to these journeymen players who were dropped by their clubs long before the expiration of their contracts.

In 1986 the devastating effects of signing free agents to long-term contracts finally made its mark upon the owners. Suddenly there was a curious and almost total lack of interest by all the owners in free agents, even in such proven players as Jack Morris, Tim Raines, and Andre Dawson. This abstention of interest brought the Players Association into action, charging the owners with collusion, conspiracy, and other high crimes. The players won the argument through special arbitration, which will result in numerous free agencies for players and huge money penalties against the owners.

The most valuable option for players today is the right to arbitrate their salary disputes. This is not the ordinary sort of arbitration in which the arbitrator has some latitude in modifying the demands or expectations of the parties in an attempt to arrive at an equitable decision.

In baseball, salary disputes between ball clubs and players are arbitrated under bizarre limitations. Each side proposes what a player's salary should be. The arbitrator is restricted to selecting one figure or the other. He has no other choice. He cannot compromise. That may seem fair enough on the surface, but in practice this procedure works for the player and against the ball club. A player may submit an excessive figure, but the ball club dares not counter with too low an offer. Thus, of necessity, a ball club's offer is often more than the player's worth or what he would normally receive if arbitration wasn't available to him. The statistics on the number of wins and losses in arbitration cases may favor the owners. As with many other statistics in baseball, however, this won-and-lost statistic is misleading. The player cannot lose even if he "loses" his case. He will become either rich or richer.

Today the money issues between the owners and the players

dominate the news, but the publication of player salaries and the financial statements of the ball clubs are not the tidings that interest the fans. What made baseball the national pastime are the competitive activities on the ball field and not the monetary squabbles in the countinghouses.

Baseball's greatest attribute is its resiliency, its inherent capacity to survive. It endured the convulsive tremors of the Federal League raids, the 1920 Black Sox scandal, the Depression, World War II, the Mexican raids, and a players' strike. It contends with perennial controversies involving the greed of the owners and the overreaching of the players. Baseball has persevered through four expansions that created an egregious imbalance in the quality of play, requiring at least five years for the teams to stabilize and become competitive again. More expansion is projected and will bring with it a recurrence of the problems of the previous expansions. Yet baseball will survive that, too.

The game is here to stay.

I N D E X

Aaron, Hank, 43, 55
Allen, Dick, 150
Allen, Richie, 49
Alston, Tom, 76
Anderson, Sparky, 82, 118
Arlett, Buzz, 80
Ashburn, Richie, 144, 151
Averill, Earl, 150

Baker, Del, 105
Balboni, Steve, 50
Baltimore Orioles, 48
Bamberger, George, 140
Banks, Ernie, 144
Bartell, Dick, 82
Barzun, Jacques, 136
Bavasi, Buzzie, 81–82, 131
Bench, Johnny, 43, 54, 116–17,
   120, 151
Benton, Al, 73–74
Berger, Wally, 42, 44, 45, 46,
   58–59, 80–81, 96
Berra, Yogi, 107, 142
Bishop, Max, 65
Blair, Paul, 151
Blue, Lu, 62
Bluege, Ossie, 61, 82–83, 93, 110,
   112–13, 138–39
Blyleven, Bert, 152
Boley, Joe, 65
Bonds, Bobby, 150
Bonura, Zeke, 80
Boone, Ike, 80
Boros, Steve, 49
Boston Braves, 45
Boston Red Sox, 12
Bottomley, Jim, 44, 150
Boyer, Ken, 151

Bridges, Tommy, 16, 98, 105, 145
Broeg, Bob, 103
Brown, Clint, 97
Brown, Lloyd, 61
Brown, Mace, 97
Buford, Don, 146
Burns, George, 5
Bush, Joe (Bullet), 16

California Angels, 12, 27, 49
Camilli, Dolf, 52, 81
Campanella, Roy, 150
Cantell, Guy, 68
Carbo, Bernie, 146
Carey, Max, 150, 151
Carlton, Steve, 152
Cash, Norm, 144, 146, 149, 150
Cavarretta, Phil, 82
Cedeno, Cesar, 150
Cey, Ron, 43, 150, 151
Chandler, Happy, 77–78, 156
Chapman, Ben, 54, 82, 92, 120,
   128–29
Chase, Hal, 151
Chicago Cubs, 126
Chicago White Sox, 1, 2, 33, 76
Cicotte, Eddie, 25
Clancy, Bud, 93
Cobb, Ty, 5, 17, 37, 64, 69, 91,
   93, 110, 113, 120, 138–39
Cochrane, Mickey, 69, 81
Colavito, Rocky, 150
Coleman, Jerry, 13
Coleman, Vince, 139
Collins, Eddie, 4–5, 17, 61, 113
Combs, Earle, 150
Comiskey, Charles, 2–3, 154
Concepcion, Dave, 151

Cooper, Mort, 145
Crandall, Del, 118
Crawford, Sam, 17, 127, 128, 144
Creamer, Robert W., 21
Cronin, Joe, 70
Crosetti, Frankie, 82
Curtis, Julian, 31
Cuyler, Kiki, 44, 45, 146, 150

Davis, Chili, 49
Davis, Curt, 98
Davis, Eric, 139
Davis, Spud, 81
Dawson, Andre, 160
Dean, Dizzy, 69, 94, 98, 145, 150, 152
Demaree, Frank, 82
DiMaggio, Joe, 37, 42, 60, 69, 81, 104, 147, 151
DiMaggio, Vince, 52
Dressen, Charlie, 105
Dreyfuss, Barney, 31–32
Dunn, Jack, 65
Durocher, Leo, 8, 142
Dykes, Jimmie, 7, 8

Earnshaw, George, 42, 65, 98
Eller, Hod, 25
Evans, Darrell, 150, 151

Faber, Harold A., 31
Faber, Red, 26, 40, 93, 145
Fain, Ferris, 49, 102–3
Falk, Bibb, 5, 33, 53, 62, 120
Feller, Bob, 53–54, 145, 152
Ferrell, Rick, 68, 81
Ferrell, Wes, 42, 145
Fitzsimmons, Freddie, 42
Ford, Russ, 25
Fox, Nellie, 13, 151
Foxx, Jimmie, 69
Frey, Lonny, 82

Friend, Bob, 133
Frisch, Frankie, 44, 85, 146

Gaedel, Eddie, 149
Galan, Augie, 81
Garagiola, Joe, 16
Gehrig, Lou, 18, 19, 43, 69, 81, 84, 98
Gehringer, Charlie, 69, 151
Glazner, Whitey, 68
Gomez, Lefty, 98, 145, 150
Gooden, Dwight, 152
Goodman, Billy, 13
Goodman, Ival, 81
Gordon, Joe, 151
Goslin, Goose, 144
Gossage, Goose, 97
Graham, Jack, 76
Gray, Pete, 156
Greenberg, Hank, 33, 55, 60, 69, 70, 81, 84, 88–89, 100, 103–4, 105–6, 111–12, 114, 147, 149
Griffith, Clark, 154
Grimes, Burleigh, 26, 42, 70
Grote, Jerry, 116
Grove, Bob, 42, 53, 65, 69, 98, 115, 152
Guidry, Ron, 16, 153

Hack, Stan, 82
Hafey, Chick, 44, 146, 150
Haines, Jess, 42, 70, 150
Hallahan, Bill, 42
Harder, Mel, 42, 98
Haregrove, Mike, 146, 148, 149, 150
Harris, Bucky, 8, 93–94, 104
Harshman, Jack, 75
Hartnett, Gabby, 44, 69, 121, 146
Hegan, Jim, 118
Heilman, Harry, 5, 40, 44, 144
Hemsley, Rollie, 81

Henderson, Rickey, 139
Henrich, Tommy, 68
Herman, Babe, 32, 44, 45, 46, 60, 81, 94, 113-14, 126-27
Herman, Billy, 71, 120, 146, 151
Herzog, Whitey, 13, 103, 108, 111
Heydler, John, 25
Higuera, Ted, 16
Hooper, Harry, 4, 146, 150
Hopp, Johnny, 82
Hornsby, Rogers, 17, 30, 40, 69, 85
Howser, Dick, 50
Hoyt, Waite, 40, 150
Hubbell, Carl, 42, 52, 70, 98
Hudlin, Willis, 42, 98

Jackson, Joe, 62
Jackson, Reggie, 54, 58
Jackson, Travis, 146, 150, 151
James, Bill, 142-44, 150, 153
Jensen, Woody, 82
John, Tommy, 152
Johnson, Ban, 25
Johnson, Sylvester, 62
Johnson, Walter, 17, 53, 69, 74, 98, 152
Joiner, Roy, 126
Jolley, Smead, 80
Jones, Sad Sam, 112
Jonnard, Claude, 68
Judd, Ralph, 68
Judge, Joe, 112

Kamm, Willie, 82, 83, 93, 114, 151
Kansas City Royals, 50, 108
Kell, George, 150
Keller, Charlie, 145
Kelly, George, 40
Kemp, Steve, 153
Kerr, Johnnie, 5, 61, 107, 109

Killefer, Bill, 126
Kiner, Ralph, 42, 48, 59, 88-89, 101-2, 145, 157
Klein, Chuck, 44, 120, 145
Klem, Bill, 129-30
Koppett, Leonard, 17
Koufax, Sandy, 52, 145, 150, 152
Koy, Ernie (Chief), 94-95
Kralik, Doug, 34
Kremer, Ray, 42
Kremer, Wiz, 127
Kuhel, Joe, 112

Lajoie, Nap, 17
Landis, Kennesaw Mountain, 3, 67-69, 154
Lanigan, Ernest, 137
Lawless, Tom, 99-100
Leach, Tommy, 23
Leiber, Hank, 81
Lemon, Bob, 84, 118, 119
Lewis, Buddy, 53-54
Lewis, J. Norman, 157
Lindstrom, Fred, 44, 150
Lopez, Al, 46, 49-50, 60, 81, 101, 119-20, 121, 126, 129-30
Los Angeles Dodgers, 132
Luciano, Ron, 125, 132
Luque, Dolf, 127
Lyons, Ted, 42

Mack, Connie, 65, 102, 154, 155
Mamaux, Al, 94, 95
Mancuso, Gus, 81
Mantle, Mickey, 18, 43, 55-57
Manush, Heinie, 68, 146, 150
Maranville, Rabbit, 40
Marberry, Firpo, 42, 97
Marichal, Juan, 145
Marion, Marty, 151, 157
Maris, Roger, 18, 43
Marquard, Rube, 145

Martin, Billy, 107, 142
Martin, Mike, 53
Mathewson, Christy, 17, 30
Mattingly, Don, 152
Mauch, Gene, 103, 125
Mays, Carl, 92, 145
Mays, Willie, 147, 151
Mazeroski, Bill, 15
McCarthy, Joe, 106
McCarver, Tim, 117, 120–21
McClain, Larry, 34
McCormick, Mike, 68
McGee, Willie, 100
McGraw, John, 85, 102, 126
McKain, Hal, 68
McMillan, Roy, 151
Merkle, Fred, 99
Meusel, Bob, 30
Miller, Marvin, 159
Minnesota Twins, 99
Mitchell, Clarence, 26, 126
Moore, Terry, 82
Moore, Wilcy, 97
Morris, Jack, 160
Morrison, Johnny (Jughandle),
    97–98
Mostil, Johnny, 5
Mungo, Van, 98
Murphy, Johnny, 97, 157
Murphy, Robert, 157
Myer, Buddy, 7

Neun, Johnny, 62
New York Giants, 27, 76, 81, 85,
    126
New York Yankees, 55, 98, 129,
    152–53
Niekro, Phil, 152
North, Bill, 146
Nunamaker, Les, 75

Oberkfell, Ken, 13

O'Connor, Leslie, 67, 68
O'Doul, Lefty, 8, 44, 102, 120
O'Farrell, Bob, 81
O'Malley, Walter, 77, 132–34
Ott, Mel, 44, 60, 69
Owen, Marv, 82

Palmer, Jim, 62
Partridge, Jay, 68
Pascual, Camilo, 16
Patek, Freddie, 12
Peckinpaugh, Roger, 32
Philadelphia Athletics, 30, 65, 98,
    113
Pierce, Billy, 16
Pillette, Herman (Old Folks),
    91–92, 127–28
Pittsburgh Pirates, 86, 133
Plank, Eddie, 145
Powell, Jake, 129
Pytlak, Frankie, 81

Quinn, John, 26

Raines, Tim, 139, 160
Reese, Jimmie, 27, 61, 98, 109,
    113, 115
Reese, Peewee, 151
Renna, Bill, 13
Rettemund, Merv, 146
Reuther, Dutch, 126
Reynolds, Allie, 145, 157
Rice, Sam, 150
Richardson, Bobby, 151
Rickey, Branch, 17–18, 27, 59,
    66–67, 80, 92, 96, 97, 100–102,
    155, 157
Rigney, John, 95
Rivers, Mickey, 149
Rixey, Eppa, 40, 150
Roberts, Robin, 145
Robinson, Brooks, 145, 151

Robinson, Floyd, 76
Robinson, Jackie, 139, 157
Rogell, Billy, 3–4
Rogers, Steve, 152
Rose, Pete, 9, 37
Roush, Edd, 146, 150
Ruel, Muddy, 81, 113
Ruffing, Red, 42, 98, 145
Ruppert, Jake, 155
Russell, Jack, 7
Ruth, Babe, 17–22, 26, 27–29, 37,
    39, 43, 55, 57–58, 61, 64, 65,
    69, 98, 114, 115, 147, 154
Ryan, Nolan, 145, 152

Saint Louis Browns, 156
Saint Louis Cardinals, 65, 66, 76,
    85, 99, 108
Samuel, Juan, 139
San Diego Padres, 8, 13, 42, 91,
    127
Santo, Ron, 150
Schalk, Ray, 150
Schmidt, Mike, 43, 54
Scott, Mike, 152
Seaver, Tom, 116, 152
Sewell, Joe, 146
Sewell, Luke, 81
Sewell, Rip, 127
Shantz, Bobby, 16
Shellenback, Frank, 8
Shibe, Thomas, 30
Shocker, Urban, 26
Simmons, Al, 7, 69, 145, 146
Simons, Mel, 68
Sisler, George, 17, 40, 44, 145–47,
    149
Smalley, Roy, 150
Smith, Lee, 97
Smith, Ozzie, 15, 110–11
Smith, Reggie, 150
Snider, Duke, 145

Speaker, Tris, 5, 17, 69, 71, 151
Spencer, Roy, 68
Stargell, Willie, 86
Starr, Bill, 8
Starr, Dave, 71
Statz, Jigger, 27, 86, 106–7, 126
Staub, Rusty, 150
Stengel, Casey, 142
Stieb, Dave, 153
Suhr, Gus, 82
Sundberg, Jim, 108–9
Sweeney, Bill, 128

Tanner, Chuck, 141
Tebbetts, Birdie, 117
Templeton, Gary, 151
Tenace, Gene, 146, 148, 149, 150
Terry, Bill, 44, 145, 147, 149
Travis, Cecil, 54
Traynor, Pie, 44, 146, 150
Trosky, Hal, 82
Trout, Dizzy, 145

Vance, Dazzy, 42, 70, 98, 145
Van Slyke, 108
Veeck, Bill, 149
Viola, Frank, 99

Waddell, Rube, 145
Wagner, Honus, 17
Walberg, Rube, 98
Walker, Bill, 42
Walker, Tillie, 30
Walsh, Ed, 17
Walters, Bucky, 145
Waner, Lloyd, 150
Waner brothers, 43, 44, 69
Warneke, Lon, 98
Washington Senators, 53
Weaver, Earl, 48, 50
Werber, Billy, 88
Westrum, Wes, 119

Wheat, Zack, 17, 145, 146
White, Jo-Jo, 120
Whitehill, Earl, 42, 87–88
Williams, Cy, 30
Williams, Dick, 140
Williams, Ken, 30
Williams, Ted, 8, 55, 57, 69, 115, 147–48
Wills, Bump, 151
Wills, Maury, 134
Wilson, Hack, 13–14, 29, 46, 150
Wilson, Jimmie, 81
Wilson, Owen, 23
Wilson, Willie, 149
Winfield, Dave, 42, 139

Wingard, Ernie, 68
Worrell, Todd, 97
Wright, Glenn, 44, 83, 87, 88
Wrigley, William, 155
Wynn, Early, 145, 150
Wynn, Jim, 150

Yastrzemski, Carl, 54, 55
York, Rudy, 105
Young, Cy, 17
Youngs, Ross, 27, 150

Zachary, Tom, 129–30
Zeller, Jack, 68
Zwilling, Dutch, 114